the assault on local government

D0060952

Andrew Sancton

Published for the City of Westmount by

McGill-Queen's University Press
Montreal & Kingston · London · Ithaca

ISBN 0-7735-2140-2 (cloth)
ISBN 0-7735-2163-1 (paper)
Legal deposit second quarter 2000

Bibliothèque nationale du Québec

Printed in Canada on acid-free paper

McGill-Queen's University Press acknowledges the financial support of the Government of Canada through the Book Publishing Industry Development Program (BPIDP) for its activities. It also acknowledges the support of the Canada Council for the Arts for its publishing program.

Canadian Cataloguing in Publication Data

Sancton, Andrew, 1948-
    Merger mania: the assault on local government

Includes bibliographical references
ISBN 0-7735-2140-2 (bnd)
ISBN 7735-2163-1 (pbk)

1. Annexation (Municipal government)
2. Annexation (Municipal government) - Case studies
3. Municipal government.   I. Title

JS78.S26 2000   320.8'59   C00-900292-8

Available in French under the title
La Frénésie des fusions: une attaque à la démocratie locale
ISBN 0-7735-2165-8

ACKNOWLEDGEMENTS

T his book was commissioned by the city of Westmount, Quebec during a time of considerable controversy about municipal boundaries in the Montreal area. As a contribution to the public discussion, I was asked to write about municipal amalgamations in Western democracies. Because many such amalgamations – most notably in Toronto – have recently been extremely topical in Ontario, the experience in this province receives considerable attention. My hope is, however, that the book will also be of interest to readers outside Quebec and Ontario who are concerned about preserving and improving systems of local government in which locally-elected councils can help determine what happens in their own local communities.

The structure, form, and content of this book are mine. In some parts, the subject matter is relatively new to me. In others, I have written about matters with which I was more familiar. The new parts – mostly historical – have enabled me to approach this subject in the most comprehensive way I know how.

Mayor Peter Trent of Westmount launched this project with a telephone call many months ago. Ever since, he has acted like a good editor for an academic publishing house: always ready with suggestions and ideas, but never insisting on one particular direction; always constructively critical, but never getting in the way of what I wanted to communicate. So concerned was he that this be a credible contribution to an important debate that he asked Professor Jean-Pierre Collin of the *Institut nationale de la recherche scientifique - Urbanisation* to act as an external reviewer. Professor Collin's thoughtful review helped me to avoid a number of errors, to clarify points that were unclear, and to learn about some important sources with which I was not previously familiar.

At city hall in Westmount, I received the friendly administrative support of Bruce St. Louis, the city's director-general. Marie-France Paquet, manager of legal services and city clerk shared with me her remarkable collection of materials from around the world about municipal amalgamation. Andrew Ross, research assistant, helped me track down a number of important items and shared in the work of constructing the table showing the number of municipalities in various American metropolitan areas. Luc Ménard, Director of Finance, generously shared his insights. Ann Moffat and the Westmount Public Library staff gave freely of their time and finally, my thanks to Marie José Aubertin for her support.

Lionel Feldman, president of Lionel Feldman Consulting Ltd., assisted me with Chapter 5 on Toronto's "Megacity." Our frequent conversations about this chapter and other aspects of the project were always helpful and reassuring.

This manuscript was written at my home in London during a much appreciated sabbatical leave from the University of Western Ontario. My family – Pam, Rebecca, and Derek – put up with papers spread over places where they could, in more normal circumstances, walk unimpeded. They also tolerated a husband and father who was often more distracted than usual. Thank you all for your patience.

While in Westmount to discuss the project, I stayed with my parents, John and Mary Sancton, sources of much personal inspiration, intellectual and otherwise. I have absorbed my father's views on the subject of this book since I was a teenager. Only later did I learn that they were consistent (but not congruent) with the theoretical framework known as "public-choice," a subject I discuss in Chapter 3. A complementary intellectual influence is the work of L. J. Sharpe, my mentor (and Lionel Feldman's) at Oxford University. Jim Sharpe's approach to local government is decidedly not rooted in the assumptions of "public choice," nor do I think is mine.

I make use of "public choice" analysis because it has been so influential in the United States and because I believe it helps counter the outlandish claims – often from people who say they believe in the innovative benefits of competition – that huge monopolistic municipalities will be more efficient and effective than a number of small ones. To glimpse my own strongly held views on why "merger mania" is wrong, I refer the reader to the last chapter of this book, especially the last paragraphs. I am much more interested in building institutions that enable citizens collectively to control some aspects of their lives outside the structures of huge governments (be they federal, provincial, or municipal) than I am with measuring efficiencies in local service delivery. If this makes me a hopelessly old-fashioned, idealistic liberal, than so be it.

Despite the city of Westmount's commission of this study, the contents and opinions expressed in it are mine, and I alone take full responsibility for them.

Andrew Sancton
London, Ontario
February, 2000

TABLE OF CONTENTS

SUMMARY

MERGER MANIA: THE ASSAULT ON LOCAL GOVERNMENT

T he purpose of the report is to analyse the advantages and disadvantages of municipal amalgamations, provide a historical perspective of such amalgamations, and examine how these experiences apply to the city-region of Montreal. The distinct characteristics of the cities studied indicate that any attempt to define one ideal size of a city-region or one ideal form of governance would be doomed to failure. Relatively small city-regions may benefit from amalgamation. Larger regions may need amalgamation of major services such as sewage treatment and public transit, but smaller municipalities provide better community services such as recreation. For city-regions the size of Montreal, amalgamation is not a likely solution. For good reasons, a single municipality stretching from Mirabel to Chambly and from Vaudreuil to Repentigny is not on anyone's agenda.

Apart from a few politicians and some public servants concerned with municipal affairs, few serious thinkers in recent years have considered it desirable to reduce the number of municipalities within city-regions. Although the consolidationist debate dates back to the 19th century, there is little contemporary support for a public policy of forced municipal amalgamations. In the past few decades, policies of "public choice" and "new regionalism" have largely supplanted the consolidationist approach. The report examines these trends from the first, consensual merger in Philadelphia up to the recent forced mergers in Nova Scotia and Ontario. The final chapter looks at these issues in relation to the city-region of Montreal.

1. MUNICIPAL AMALGAMATION IN THE UNITED STATES, 1854-1942

Current debates in Canada about municipal amalgamations frequently cite American references, both positive and negative, and indeed the United States has had some influence on the structure and practice of local governments in Canada. It is important, however, to remember one big difference – American municipalities enjoy constitutional protection from coercion by state governments. A municipal corporation in the United States is created mainly for the interest, advantages and convenience of the locality and its people. American cities grow by annexing unincorporated areas within their counties and no solvent American municipality has been forced, against its will, to lose its status and join another in almost 100 years. The amalgamations of distinct municipalities that did occur did so following approval by referendum. The two most dramatic examples are Philadelphia and New York.

The amalgamation of Philadelphia, in 1854, involved the merger of an entire county and all its municipalities. In institutional terms, it was not unlike the recent merger of Metro Toronto and its six constituent municipalities. Conceived in response to a serious social problem – the breakdown of law and order – amalgamation enjoyed considerable support among the political elite. Despite great optimism that the amalgamation would yield many benefits, it actually only addressed the policing problem. Otherwise, bigness brought weakness and corruption rather than imagination and quality of service, and did nothing to stop Philadelphia's economic decline.

The most significant municipal consolidation ever undertaken in North America was New York's in 1898. In that year fifteen cities and towns and eleven villages in five separate counties were merged to form the new city of New York, with a population of 3.5 million. New York was already a major world city, and a century later it is the world's paramount economic centre. Manhattan has remained a home base for the world's rich and famous, but the other municipalities, such as Queen's and the Bronx, did not fare so well.

The movement for consolidation in New York was spurred by some business interests concerned that the city's economic growth was not keeping pace with that of more westerly cities, notably Chicago. They believed that "if a single municipal government could gain control over New York harbour and all the surrounding territory, it could promote the unified, comprehensive development of shipping, railroads, and related facilities in such a way as to aid both merchants and property owners." One proponent insisted that "New York was in competition with London, Paris, Chicago, and even Brooklyn... and all these had grown by increasing their boundaries; consolidation would enable the city to hold its own" – a debatable claim akin to today's global competition clichés.

In 1894, the New York State legislature enacted a law providing for a referendum on consolidation. The greatest opposition came from the city of Brooklyn where anti-consolidationists were concerned with identity and local control, though pro-consolidationists in Brooklyn argued that a share of Manhattan's tax base would lower Brooklyn's tax rates and provide better services. The prospect of a tax grab by Brooklyn, in turn, stirred opposition in Manhattan. In any event, the referendum carried in all the counties, but only by a vote of 64,744 to 64,467 in Brooklyn.

Amalgamation in New York did not save money. In the ten years following consolidation there was a sharp upward trend in expenditures and funded debt. Budget appropriations for the city increased from $78.4 million in 1898, to $98.6 million in 1903, and to $130.4 million in 1907. Between 1896 and 1899, tax rates in Manhattan went up by about sixteen per cent, due largely to consolidation.

During the 20th century there was significant public investment in New York's infrastructure – especially for transportation – but most planning and investments came from a remarkable network of special-purpose authorities that transcended the city's boundaries (the New York State Metropolitan Transportation Authority and the Port Authority of New York and New Jersey).

A century later, New York is by far the most populous municipality in the United States with a population twice the size of its old rival, Chicago, and comprises fully half of the greater New York City region compared to Chicago's one-quarter of its region. Yet it was New York that was bankrupt in the mid-1970s, not Chicago.

Since 1898, there have been no more comprehensive legislated municipal amalgamations in the United States. In most states such legislation would violate the state constitution. At a minimum, popular approval through referenda in affected municipalities would be required.

2. THE ERA OF BIG GOVERNMENT: THE 1960S AND 70S

After 1945, there was great faith in the ability of government to solve problems. Part of this government-centred solution involved "modernizing"

9

small municipalities that seemed hopelessly out of touch with the spirit of the times.

In England in the late 1950s, a royal commission did an extensive study of local government in the London region which led to the establishment, in 1964, of the upper-tier Greater London Council (GLC). The 32 boroughs comprising Greater London retained their own mayor and council. These municipalities – together with the city of London – still exist today, with the same boundaries that came into being in 1964. The GLC, however, does not.

In the 1960s, local government in the rest of England was studied, and despite the fact that there were no economies of scale to be gained, amalgamations were enacted anyway. Between 1960 and 1975, the total number of municipalities was reduced from 1349 to 521.

In 1953 the Municipality of Metropolitan Toronto (Metro) came into being as North America's first upper-tier multi-functional urban government. It comprised thirteen lower-tier constituent units. For many years to come Toronto's metro system would be much admired and studied throughout the world as a model of governmental arrangements for city-regions. By all accounts it was an outstanding success, using the city's lucrative tax base to fund infrastructure development in the far-flung urbanizing townships. In 1966, the number of constituent municipalities in Metro was reduced to six. Meanwhile, most of the growth was taking place outside Metro's borders (as was the case with the Montreal Urban Community, established in 1969).

The most comprehensive single merger in North America since New York in 1898 took place in 1965 on Ile-Jésus, just north of Montreal, when fourteen municipalities were merged to form the new city of Laval, Quebec's second most populous municipality. A significant motivating factor in this merger was the desire to prevent land speculation and haphazard development on valuable farmland. But it was legislation sponsored by the *parti québecois*, the *Agricultural Land Preservation Act* of 1978, and possibly a slower growth than was anticipated, that turned out to be more important in preventing urban sprawl. Meanwhile, there is no evidence that the Laval amalgamation has saved money or resulted in a higher quality of urban infrastructure.

The comprehensive amalgamation in 1972 in Winnipeg, the Unicity, has received a lot of attention because it was accompanied by innovative mechanisms to enhance local community involvement and participation. Such mechanisms have since all been disbanded. Planners had assumed that by equalizing tax levels and services, the relatively well off suburbs would subsidize the revitalization of the central city. However a 1980 study demonstrated that that the Unicity structure, with its many suburban councillors and large tax base, facilitated the building of suburban infrastructure instead, to the detriment of inner-city investment. After 30 years, there is once again a need for new mechanisms for regional co-operation, resulting in the creation of a Capital Region Committee. No one is talking of further amalgamation.

Municipal amalgamation was also popular in continental Europe during this period. In many such countries, municipalities deliver most of public welfare services. The countries in which there were the most significant reductions in the number of municipalities were: Sweden (2500 in 1950, 279 in 1980); Denmark (1387 in 1961, 275 in 1974); and West Germany (24,512 in 1959, 8514 in 1978). But not all of Europe, any more than all of Canada, was swept up in amalgamation frenzy. In 1950, Italy had 7810 municipalities, in 1972 there were 8056; Greece had 5993 in 1962 and 6037 in 1979; France had 37,708 in 1968 and 36,423 in 1980. Where there were few amalgamations, new mechanisms for regional co-operation were usually established.

3. The Decline of the Consolidationist Movement In The United States, the Emergence of "Public Choice," and "New Regionalism"

In current political debate in Canada about municipal structures, there are frequent references to the American experience, many of them misleading or outrightly false. For example, it is often thought that Montreal is unusual in having 111 municipalities within its census metropolitan area. In comparison to American metropolitan areas of similar size, however, this figure is well within the norm. The American debate is between public-choice advocates and "new regionalists" who, unlike the consolidationists before them, advocate independent municipalities combined with loose regional institutions. Merging into one large city creates a monopoly. Independent municipalities, while allowing for regional co-operation, promote choice and competition. There are three conclusions to be drawn from this chapter:

- First, throughout most of the twentieth century, there have been no comprehensive municipal amalgamations in the United States as we understand the concept in Canada.
- Second, public-choice analysis shows us that the efficient delivery of municipal services does not require large municipalities.

11

- Third, a reading of the "new regionalist" literature in the United States should teach us that the problem with Canadian city-regions is not that they are deficient in formal municipal structures or that they lack provincial involvement.

Most American "new regionalists" would be favourably impressed by both the existence of the Montreal Urban Community (MUC) and by the policies of the Quebec government in protecting farmland. What is missing in Montreal – and other Canadian cities – is an understanding that the economic and social health of our cities is a responsibility of all those with the resources to bring about change. Improving the quality of life in our city-regions is not just a responsibility of those who sit on municipal councils or in provincial legislatures. It is equally a responsibility of the major economic interests based in our various urban areas. Incorporating such interests into our urban policy-making processes without surrendering the final decision-making authority of elected politicians is an extremely delicate undertaking. But it is a process that will ultimately be far more productive than our continuous battles about ideal structures and boundaries for municipal government.

4. AMALGAMATIONS IN THE 1990S

For some central governments in the 1990s, municipal amalgamations were back on the agenda but this time the priorities were different. The aim now is to reduce the size of government and to promote economic development. Relatively little is heard about how amalgamations could equalize services and taxes and facilitate regional planning and infrastructure development. Unlike the situation in the 1960s and 1970s, the amalgamations of the 1990s seem isolated to only a very few jurisdictions.

The restructuring of local government in New Zealand in 1989 accompanied a complete overhaul of the national government, one so extensive that it has attracted a great deal of attention for a country with a population of only 3.6 million. Prior to 1989, New Zealand had no intermediate level of government between the national government and the local. As a result, although the 1989 reforms reduced the number of municipalities from 249 to 74, they also established twelve directly elected regional councils whose functions are mainly concerned with the regulation of the natural environment. Reforms in New Zealand were very much concerned with decentralization. Nevertheless, police, fire protection, and public education remain as national-government functions, perhaps because, by Canadian standards, population levels are low. The largest regional council, Auckland, has a population of 982,000 while the smallest has only 33,000. Within Auckland region, the population of the central city is only 321,000, even after all the restructuring.

As in New Zealand, local governments in Australia do not do very much. There is no local spending or control for police or public education. In fact, the main institutions of urban government in Australia are the state governments and their associated public authorities. Despite their relative lack of functional strength, Australian municipalities have been constantly subjected to pressure from state governments to amalgamate with each other. In recent years, the issue has been especially controversial but despite popular protest, the amalgamations were implemented. Studies show that savings, if any, are accompanied by failure to maintain infrastructure, and local communities have not made any substantial economic gains. In the Sydney city-region, comprising 45 municipalities, there have been no consolidations for several decades, yet the largest city, Blacktown, has a population of 244,176 and the central city, Sydney, a population of 19,913.

In Britain, Margaret Thatcher's policy was to abolish upper-tier authorities, not to amalgamate lower-tier ones. Under Prime Minister Major, amalgamations occurred, usually accompanied by the amalgamated units leaving the jurisdiction of an upper-tier authority. Although Prime Minister Blair is establishing a new authority for metropolitan London, he emphasizes that its administrative structure will be very light. There will be no lower-tier amalgamations.

Except for Toronto, the most important recent Canadian amalgamation was in Halifax in 1996. Transition costs were originally estimated at $10 million, they were actually $26 million. Modest operational cost savings were projected, but none have materialized. Financial analysis is extremely difficult, in part because of the administrative confusion caused by the transition process. The amalgamation is not popular. Labour conflicts have been serious, but wage levels have generally been raised to those of the highest-paying former municipality. A recent survey in 1999 shows that 66 per cent of Haligonians are still opposed to amalgamation, three years after the event. Amalgamation is now defended on the grounds that it promotes economic development, but no case has been made concerning why businesses might prefer locating in a large municipality rather than a small one, when other factors are held constant.

Since the mid-1980s, Ontario governments led by premiers from each of the three political parties have promoted municipal amalgamation. Only the Harris government has caused large numbers of amalgamations to be implemented. Prior to 1995, there were 815 municipalities in Ontario. As of August 1999, the Harris Conservatives take credit for reducing the number of municipalities by 229 (28 per cent) and the number of elected municipal officials by 1059 (23 per cent), despite previous assertions that big government was not better and that services always cost more in larger communities.

The central governments in Victoria (Australia), Nova Scotia, and Ontario clearly believe that municipal politicians and municipalities are inherently wasteful, inefficient, and incapable of co-operating with each other. Notwithstanding evidence to the contrary, their solution is to try to save money and promote economic development by creating bigger municipalities governed by fewer elected councillors. Not all public-policy decisions are taken on the basis of careful and rational evaluations of alternative courses of action or inaction.

5. TORONTO'S MEGACITY

The biggest amalgamation since that of New York in 1898 was that of Toronto in 1998. When Premier Harris came to office in 1995, he appeared to be committed to getting rid of the upper tier in Metro Toronto's two-tier system. For reasons that are still unclear, by late 1996 his government chose total amalgamation as the means of reaching this objective, even though no one inside or outside the Conservative party had been recommending it and despite massive protests and negative referendum results.

The primary justification for the megacity was that it would save money. In December 1996, when the policy was first announced, the minister of municipal affairs claimed that, after three years, Toronto's amalgamation would save $300 million annually. A year later he was down to $240 million. A year-and-a-half after that, the city of Toronto was claiming $150 million in annual savings. Now the evidence suggests that any savings from amalgamation are highly unlikely. Two or three years from now – when all the details of new collective agreements have been worked out – it might well be possible to document the net costs of amalgamation.

As a political institution, Toronto's new city council has worked much more effectively than anyone expected. This is primarily due to the leadership of Mayor Mel Lastman. Without a strong executive committee and a local party system, Mayor Lastman has built personal support by staunchly defending the city's financial interests against various provincial initiatives. He is in an exceptionally strong position because the provincial government needs to be able to continue to show that the megacity is successful.

Because the government's own measure of success for the megacity was the saving of money and the prevention of municipal tax increases within Toronto, Mayor Lastman has been very successful in wringing financial concessions from the province. As recently as 24 November 1999, Ontario's minister of municipal affairs was stating that "the amalgamation of Toronto has been a success due to the savings that have been achieved." Since there is now evidence there will be no savings, does it therefore follow that the sponsors of megacity will one day acknowledge that their policy failed?

6. MORE CHANGE IN ONTARIO: OTTAWA, HAMILTON, SUDBURY AND TORONTO (AGAIN)

Municipal restructuring was not a significant issue in the June 1999 Ontario provincial election. In the Conservatives' election platform, Blueprint, there was only one reference to the subject. Stating that "We have found plenty of common sense ways to cut government waste and improve efficiency," it cited the following example: "Reducing the number of municipalities and school boards, resulting in more than 2200 fewer municipal politicians." There were no other references – nothing about Toronto, about regional governments, or about the desirability of further amalgamations. In fact, Conservative candidates in suburban areas tended to state that there would be no forced amalgamations in their areas. However, less than three months after the election, the new minister of municipal affairs announced that he was taking action "to protect taxpayers in the Regional Municipalities of Haldimand-Norfolk, Hamilton-Wentworth, Ottawa-Carleton and Sudbury from the costs of large bureaucracy, increased red tape and inefficient municipal government." In each of these areas there had been years of conflict between the two tiers of municipal government and many attempts at reorganization.

In September, the minister appointed a special advisor for each area with instructions to report back in 60 days with recommendations for a new organizational structure that would result in:

• Fewer municipal politicians

15

- Lower taxes
- A better and more efficient delivery of services
- Less bureaucracy, and
- Clear lines of responsibility and better accountability at the local level

The special advisors in Ottawa, Hamilton, and Sudbury each recommended total amalgamation, in large measure because they claimed it would save money. The government then prepared legislation to implement the amalgamations, but it included none of the unique recommendations proposed by the advisors for each particular city, such as that Ottawa be declared officially bilingual. Instead the government seemed more concerned with making concessions to its own outraged suburban supporters.

The same legislation, known as the Fewer Municipal Politicians Act, also contained provisions to reduce the size of the Toronto city council from 58 to 45. Until a few days before the announcement, no one knew that such a change was on the agenda.

When a provincial government's main objective is to reduce the number of municipal politicians, it can achieve its objective by: 1) amalgamating municipalities; and/or 2) legislating a reduction in council size. Concentrating on this, the Ontario government ignored the serious debate in Toronto on important issues such as regional planning, city-suburban equity and, in some cases, the difficult choices between the benefits of being small and the benefits of being big. In the other regions, the debate was cut off before it could start. Anyone concerned with the effective governance of complex city-regions in the early twenty-first century has little to learn from events in Ontario in late 1999.

CONCLUSION: WHAT PROBLEMS IN MONTREAL ARE MUNICIPAL AMALGATIONS SUPPOSED TO SOLVE?

Mayor Bourque's proposal to amalgamate all the MUC municipalities bears some resemblance to the Ontario government's megacity policy for Toronto. In both cases a large, dominant central-city municipality would be formed within an even larger city-region. Mayor Bourque advocates enlarging the MUC (but without a policing function), thereby creating a relatively strong upper-tier government for the entire Montreal metropolitan region. Ironically, if the Harris government had been willing to establish such an upper-tier authority for the Greater Toronto Area (GTA), it is highly unlikely it ever would have adopted a megacity policy. But Mayor Bourque seems to want large-scale amalgamation and a strong upper-tier authority. The great weakness in both Mayor Bourque's position and that of the Harris government, is that neither is able to show how the creation of one overwhelmingly dominant municipality within a city-region is likely to enhance regional co-operation, with or without a powerful upper-tier council. This is a serious weakness, because all the studies of municipal problems in the GTA and in Greater Montreal have pointed to the urgent need to promote such co-operation, not to establish a giant central city.

There are three important differences in the governmental and political environment in the pre-megacity Toronto city-region and in today's Montreal city-region:

1. The city of Montreal (population 1.0 million) is already more dominant within the Montreal Urban Community (1.8 million) than the old city of Toronto (0.7 million) was within Metro (2.4 million). This no doubt explains why the old city of Toronto was a fervent opponent of Toronto's megacity while the current city of Montreal favours a megacity for Montreal. One of the central motivations of the Harris government was to eliminate the political and administrative extravagances that it perceived in the old city of Toronto. It is, however, hard to see how an amalgamated MUC would be anything other than a complete takeover by the city of Montreal. Regardless of whether or not a Montreal takeover would be good public policy, everyone should at least acknowledge that such an end result is the exact opposite of what the megacity in Toronto was all about.

2. There were six constituent municipalities in Metro Toronto. There are 28 in the MUC. The complexities and expenses of the Toronto amalgamation would seem minor in comparison to a Montreal amalgamation. For example, all municipal employees in Ontario belong to one pension plan, the Ontario Municipal Employee Retirement System (OMERS). Within the MUC, each municipality has its own pension plan. Setting up retirement packages and standardizing pension arrangements after an MUC amalgamation would be an administrative and financial nightmare. The only way to simplify the transition in Montreal would be to eliminate the suburban workforce and to establish everywhere the administrative procedures and practices of Montreal. Such a policy would guarantee significant increases in costs and also severely challenge the city of Montreal's management capacity.

3. Municipal political parties were not – and are not – a factor in Toronto. In the MUC they exist in some municipalities and not in others. It is hard to imagine that they would not exist in an amalgamated island city. Has anyone given any thought to the implications of establishing a single municipal party system throughout a Montreal megacity? As a result, many people who currently are willing to serve on suburban municipal councils would be less likely to run for office, or the current parties would be relatively weaker within the new council. How well would the new city council function in the absence of a majority party? Will a new mayor of an amalgamated Montreal ever be in as strong a political position as Mel Lastman has been in Toronto?

It is extremely difficult to understand the arguments in favour of an amalgamated MUC. In Toronto, the provincial government wanted to get rid of one tier of directly-elected municipal government. This is not an issue in Montreal, because MUC councillors have never been directly elected to serve only at that level. Saving money appears not be a strong motivating factor in Montreal. In any event, experience in Toronto and elsewhere should quickly disabuse anyone of the notion that an amalgamation on this scale will save money. Similarly, no one in Quebec seems as concerned as the Harris government was about reducing the number of elected politicians. Does anyone seriously believe that members of councils for suburban municipalities within the MUC are somehow a drain on the public purse?

Arguments based on concerns about economic development miss the point. If they were relevant, they would apply to the entire city-region. Of course, there is a need to promote Montreal throughout the world. But all municipalities in the region should be involved, not just those on the island of Montreal. As countless American city-regions have proved, city-regions can grow, prosper, and breed innovation when there are dozens or even hundreds of municipalities. Municipal amalgamation has nothing to do with economic development.

Social equity is not addressed by analgamation. No one wants to promote or defend a system of municipal government that favours the rich and places undue burdens on the poor. Unlike the situation in Ontario, Quebec municipalities have virtually no role in social services and none in relation to income security. Wealthy Montrealers cannot escape paying for social services and welfare by moving to a suburb. Since the MUC already exists and acts as a mechanism for sharing central-city police costs, and since the province finances social services and income security, the city of

Montreal probably bears fewer costs of central-city poverty than almost any other major central city in North America.

We are left with arguments for amalgamation that are essentially little more than appeals to municipal grandeur (in the case of Mayor Bourque) or administrative tidiness (in the case of the Bédard report). But, anyone who wants to change such boundaries against the will of the people affected should be obliged to specify the precise problems for which the boundary change is the solution. The difficulty in confronting the case for municipal amalgamation within the MUC is that the problems that are allegedly to be corrected have not been specified.

Mayor Bourque has spoken and written frequently about the desirability of amalgamation. On some occasions he has made specific reference to developments elsewhere. For example, on 24 November 1999 he wrote the following in The Gazette:

> We cannot deny that we are influenced by events elsewhere in Canada. We cannot ignore the fact that mergers are taking place in Ontario and Nova Scotia. Toronto has a population of 2.4 million and Halifax close to 400,000. Even now, the Ontario government is planning additional amalgamations in Ottawa and Hamilton regions as well as in other areas. If consolidation works for Toronto and Halifax, and is being considered for Ottawa, why wouldn't it work for Montreal, Quebec City, and Sherbrooke?

The object of this report has been to enable us to place such comments in perspective.

INTRODUCTION

I n 1854, the state legislature of Pennsylvania approved a law that joined 28 nearby municipal governments to the city of Philadelphia. The result was a city of 500,000 people. Within a radius of twenty miles from downtown, only 95,000 people then lived outside the jurisdiction of the central city. In 1996, of the six million people in Philadelphia's city-region, only a quarter lived within the city itself though the boundaries remained the same as they were in 1854.[1] Many different conclusions can be drawn from these bare facts. The least contentious, perhaps, is that legislated municipal amalgamation is not a new policy, in the United States at least. Much else about the lessons from Philadelphia's story would likely be subject to heated dispute. Without focusing on Philadelphia, the aims of this report are to explore the history of municipal amalgamations in advanced liberal democracies, to analyse the longstanding disputes about the advantages and disadvantages of such amalgamations, and to draw some lessons for the city-region of Montreal.

The report is not about the ideal size of city-regions, or even about the ideal size of their component municipalities. As will become apparent later, the search for such ideals is doomed to failure. Nor is the report about ideal forms of government for city-regions, although such a concern overlaps with the issue of municipal amalgamation. For relatively small city-regions, it is possible that one amalgamated municipality might cover all or most of the urbanized territory. Amalgamation for such places might be seen by some as a solution to the problem of city-region governance. For city-regions the size of Montreal, however, such a solution is less likely. A single municipality stretching from Mirabel to Chambly and from Vaudreuil to Repentigny seems – for good reason – to be on no one's agenda.

---

1. Jon C. Teaford, *City and Suburb: The Political Fragmentation of Metropolitan America, 1850-1970* (Baltimore: Johns Hopkins University Press, 1979), pp.26 & 33; Victor Jones, *Metropolitan Government* (Chicago: University of Chicago Press, 1942). 1996 population figures are from U.S. federal census: <http:www.census.gov/Press-Release/metro01.prn> and <http://www.gov/statab/ccdb301.txt>.

Because the report is not focused on the intellectual and practical problem of how to govern city-regions within larger central government jurisdictions, it simply does not connect well with much of the recent literature about city-regions in the global economy.[2] It appears that systems of municipal government are not especially relevant to a city-region's global competitiveness, although most observers seem to agree that competitive city-regions need some kind of local institution that encompasses all or most of a city-region's territory. The fact is, however, that, apart from a few politicians and some public servants concerned with municipal affairs, few serious thinkers in recent years have paid much attention to the desirability of reducing the number of municipalities within city-regions. In most places, such a policy was assumed to be irrelevant. Because there is so little in the way of current intellectual justification for a public policy of forced municipal amalgamations, we must rely instead on a thorough understanding of its historical origins. There are, of course, some places – Nova Scotia and Ontario being the best examples – where, despite the lack of intellectual justification, municipal amalgamation has recently been in vogue. A particular concern of this report will be to explain how this came to be and to assess the early impact of what has happened.

If the report were concerned with how best to govern city-regions, there would be a rich academic literature on which to draw. The main debate is between the "consolidationists," who favour some form of metropolitan government for each city-region, and the advocates of "public choice," who point especially to the economic benefits of having small, competitive municipalities, each with its own distinct bundle of services and tax levels. The emergence of these competing viewpoints will be examined as we review the history of municipal amalgamations in the United States. The public-choice literature helps explain why municipal amalgamations are not now frequently advocated in the United States. The inheritors of the consolidationist position, which dates back to the later 19th century, are now more interested in promoting loose regional institutions rather than outright amalgamations.[3]

The report begins with a full discussion of the movement for municipal amalgamations in the United States in the second half of the 19th century, culminating in the consolidation of 1898 that created the current

---

2. See, for example, Paul L. Knox and Peter J. Taylor, eds., *World Cities in a World System* (Cambridge: Cambridge University Press, 1995).
3. A notable exception is David Rusk, a former mayor of Alburquerque, New Mexico. See his *Cities Without Suburbs*, 2nd ed. (Washington DC: Woodrow Wilson Center Press, 1995). Rusk's argument will be addressed later.

boundaries of the city of New York. This same chapter describes the movement's demise in the first half of the 20th century. Chapter 2 examines trends favouring municipal amalgamation in Europe, Britain, and Canada in the 1960s and 1970s, an era of great optimism about the capacity for government restructuring to solve society's problems. Chapter 3 returns to the United States to describe developments there since 1945. Here the emphasis is on the emergence of public-choice analysis and the recent and apparently successful efforts to rejuvenate American city-regions without amalgamating municipalities.

Chapter 4 looks at the renewed interest in municipal amalgamations in Britain, New Zealand, Australia, and parts of Canada during the 1990s. This will be an opportunity to assess, among other things, the effects of the creation of the amalgamated Halifax Regional Municipality in 1996. Chapter 5 comprehensively describes and analyses how and why Toronto's "megacity" was created in 1998. The chapter will also include the first major external attempt to assess its impact. Chapter 6 examines the most recently legislated amalgamations in Ontario: Ottawa, Hamilton and Sudbury. Finally, the conclusion of the report will apply what has been learned to the current situation in Montreal.

CHAPTER   1

MUNICIPAL AMALGAMATION IN THE UNITED STATES, 1854-1942

C urrent debates in Canada about municipal amalgamation include frequent references to the United States, both as an experience to emulate and as one to avoid. As W.B. Munro pointed out in 1929, Americans have had more influence on the structure and practice of government at the local level in Canada than at either the federal or provincial levels.[1] These are two good reasons why this report devotes considerable attention in two separate chapters to the United States. Despite their obvious similarities, however, the systems of local government in the two countries are far from identical. Before going any further, it is therefore crucially important to clarify some key relevant differences in the governmental structures of the two countries.

First, unlike Canadian provinces, American states have their own written constitutions. Most such constitutions contain references to the kind of laws state legislatures may or may not approve with respect to local governments. It is in this sense that many American municipalities are constitutionally protected, not by the American federal constitution (the one with which most Canadians are passingly familiar), but by state constitutions. Different state constitutions have different amending formulas, but in all cases it is more difficult to amend the state constitution than it is to approve an ordinary law in the state legislature.

Second, most of these same state constitutions have always included provisions relating to territorial sub-divisions, usually known as counties. Although American counties seem similar in some respects to counties that exist in some Canadian provinces, including the ones that formerly existed within Quebec, there are four important distinctions: 1) counties generally cover entire states, including uninhabited areas; 2) some areas of counties do not contain municipalities (usually known as "cities" or "towns") and such

---

1. *American Influences on Canadian Government* (Toronto: Macmillan, 1929).

areas are referred to as being "unincorporated;" 3) even when areas within counties are incorporated as municipalities, they are still subject, to some degree at least, to county jurisdiction; and 4) members of the governing bodies of counties (often known as "boards of supervisors") are generally directly elected by all residents of the county, usually in partisan (Democrats vs. Republicans) elections.

The legal distinction between counties and municipal corporations was articulated in an important decision of the Ohio Supreme Court in 1857:

> Municipal corporations proper are called into existence, either at the direct solicitation or by the free consent of the people who compose them. Counties are local subdivisions of the state, created by the sovereign power of the state, of its sovereign will, without the particular solicitation, consent, or concurrent action of the people who inhabit them... A municipal corporation proper is created mainly for the interest, advantage, and convenience of the locality and its people. A county organization is created almost exclusively with a view to the policy of the state at large, for purposes of political organization and civil administration, in matters of finance, of education, of provision for the poor, of military organization, of the means of travel and transport, and especially for the general administration of justice.[2]

What all this means for debates about municipal amalgamation is that American city-regions invariably contain one or more counties, each of which usually includes areas that are incorporated as municipalities as well as areas that are unincorporated. When Americans think about changing municipal boundaries, they are usually thinking about the annexation of unincorporated areas to existing municipalities or the creation of new municipalities. The term "city-county consolidation" means the merging of all unincorporated areas within a county with the territory of the central city. Such consolidations are not as comprehensive as large-scale municipal amalgamations in Canada because, in recent times at least, they have not included suburban cities and towns.

Some 19th-century municipal amalgamations in the United States (San Francisco in 1856, St. Louis in 1876, and Denver in 1903) involved a simultaneous enlargement of the city's territory and its separation from the

---

2. Quoted in Victor Jones, *Metropolitan Government* (Chicago: University of Chicago Press, 1942), p.213.

pre-existing county to form a new consolidated city and county.[3] Since both processes were intimately entwined, it is impossible to isolate the effects of the amalgamation. One result was clear, however: future annexations of unincorporated areas were impossible for these cities because no such areas now existed within the new jurisdiction.

CONSOLIDATION IN PHILADELPHIA, 1854

What makes the Philadelphia amalgamation, referred to in the opening sentence of this report, so relevant to today's debates in Montreal is that it involved the simultaneous merger of an entire county and all its constituent municipalities. In institutional terms, it was not unlike the recent merger of the Municipality of Metropolitan Toronto and its six constituent municipalities.

Above all, consolidation in Philadelphia was caused by an apparent breakdown in law and order. The source of the problem was ongoing conflict between working class Protestant, native-born Americans (known as "Native" Americans) and just about everybody else, especially Blacks and Irish Catholics. Riots and street violence were frequent. Culprits could easily escape apprehension by crossing municipal boundaries. The consolidation movement was begun in 1844 by a group of public-spirited Philadelphians who claimed that amalgamation would facilitate the creation of a professional police force that could cover the entire territory. The same group stated that ethnically organized volunteer fire departments in different communities need not be affected. The initial response of the city establishment was to resist consolidation, partly because they feared their inability to retain political control within the new boundaries and partly because they feared that city taxes would go up to support the needs of the poorer suburbs.[4]

After a race riot in 1849, opposition to consolidation within the city evaporated. The need for better policing arrangements seemed desperate. Equally important, "the division of the county between Democrats and their

---

3. Other cities, such as in Baltimore 1851, were separated from their respective counties, but they did not receive additional territory at the same time. See Jones, *Metropolitan Government*, pp.123-30 and Jon C. Teaford, *City and Suburb: The Political Fragmentation of Metropolitan America, 1850-1970* (Baltimore: Johns Hopkins University Press, 1979), pp.47-50.

4. Sam Bass Warner, Jr., *The Private City: Philadelphia in Three Periods of its Growth* (Philadelphia: University of Pennsyvania Press, 1968), p.152.

opponents [mainly Whigs] was so even that politicians of either camp could imagine themselves as benefiting from the amalgamation."[5] The result was that, by 1854, all major newspapers were supporting amalgamation and consolidationists were elected from Philadelphia to both the state senate and the state assembly. Not surprisingly, a wide array of arguments was marshalled in support of consolidation. Eli K. Price, the state senator from Philadelphia, presented one of the first ever projections of financial savings. He claimed that the elimination of 168 tax collectors from the different jurisdictions would save $100,000 per year. In another preview of what was often part of the consolidation chronology elsewhere, Pennsylvania's governor was roused from bed to sign the bill immediately on approval in the legislature "because certain districts were considering assuming new debts for railroad loans and similar projects, in the expectation that the consolidated city would have to pay for them."[6]

Writing in 1930, Paul Studenski, one of the earliest American scholars of metropolitan government, presaged yet another feature of consolidation disputes. Here is his analysis of the financial impact of the Philadelphia consolidation:

> [T]he change was followed by a substantial retrenchment in expenditures. But in this instance … any savings that resulted cannot be ascribed altogether to consolidation. Some might have been effected anyway, for there was a distinct shift in public sentiments from a policy of expansion of municipal activities to one of distinct contraction.[7]

By 1870, the period of "contraction" was apparently over. In that year the city eliminated the volunteer fire departments and created a single, paid department for its entire territory.[8] Consolidation in Philadelphia had earlier brought into being a professional police force, which was much needed during the tumult of the Civil War. Its make-up, carefully balanced between native-born Protestants and Irish Catholics, was a key feature of post-consolidation Philadelphia politics.

---

5. Warner, *The Private City,* p.153.
6. Elizabeth M. Geffen, "Industrial Development and Social Crisis, 1841-1854," in Russell. F. Weigley, ed., *Philadelphia: A 300-Year History* (New York: W.W. Norton, 1982), p.360
7. *The Government of Metropolitan Areas in the United States* (New York: National Municipal League, 1930) p.208.
8. Dorothy Gondos Beers, "The Centennial City, 1865-1876" in Weigley, ed. *Philadelphia,* p.438.

The new Philadelphia included about 1,500 farms and 10,000 cattle.[9] A single tax rate in all areas of the new city was quite out of the question. The *Consolidation Act of 1854* required the city to distinguish between urban and rural services and to set two different tax rates accordingly. In 1868 an additional category for "semi-rural or suburban" areas was added. Properties in this category paid two-thirds of the full urban rate; rural properties paid one half. City assessors were given the authority to determine which properties fell into which category.[10] All subsequent municipal amalgamations, including areas with different levels of municipal services, have had to confront the issue of differential tax rates.

There was much optimism in Philadelphia as a result of consolidation, but it could not be sustained. Here are two separate assessments of consolidation's long-term impact. The first was written in 1968 by Sam Bass Warner, Jr., an eminent American urban historian:

> The consolidation of all the county into one municipal corporation in 1854 brought unity of management to the major functions of government, but it did not bring with it imagination or high quality of service…
>
> Bigness and industrialization had already destroyed both the source of competent leadership and the informed community which would have been necessary for the city to have enjoyed a future of strong, efficient, and imaginative government. Instead a century of weakness and corruption lay ahead.[11]

Here is the assessment, written in 1982, of Russell F. Weigley, a professor of history at Temple University in Philadelphia:

> Its tempering of the city's violence was the consolidated government's most notable early success. Other than the police, the bureaus and departments of the municipal administration remained closely linked with the unwieldy Councils [there were two chambers], and any improvement in them did not match the hopes that the Consolidation Act might have aroused. The early mayors… were men of considerable ability; the personnel of Councils, in contrast, probably warranted the grumbling with which fastidious Philadelphians discussed them. The complexities of the new big city, along with managing the new industrial establishments, were prominent among the factors that in the nineteenth century made a political

---

9. Russell F. Weigley, "The Border City in Civil War, 1854-1865" in Weigley, ed., *Philadelphia*, p.363.
10. Studenski, *The Government of Metropolitan Areas*, p.161
11. *The Private City*, p.102.

career and business leadership more and more specialized and therefore separate occupations. Councilmen were therefore less and less prominent business, social, and civic figures than they had been.[12]

All this is not to say that the city of Philadelphia would have been better off had its boundaries remained as they were prior to 1854. Had there not been the consolidation, the city's boundaries would doubtless have expanded incrementally as those in other cities did during this period. The consolidation in Philadelphia was an ambitious act of deliberate public policy around which there was considerable agreement among political elites of the time. Apart from solving the policing problem, it appears, however, that it did little or nothing to improve the quality of local political life, to make other municipal services any more effective or efficient, or to stop Philadelphia's relative economic decline in relation to other American cities.

CONSOLIDATION IN NEW YORK, 1898

The most significant municipal consolidation ever undertaken in North America was that of New York in 1898. In that year 15 cities and towns and 11 villages in five separate counties were merged to form the new city of New York, with a population of 3.5 million. The story of New York's consolidation contains many twists and turns, and comprises most of the factors with which we are familiar in today's debates – except the claim that it would reduce overall municipal expenditures. Its long-term lessons are far from clear. New York was a major world city in 1898. A century later it is the world's paramount economic centre. Did consolidation make a difference? Throughout the past 100 years, Manhattan – unlike other centre-city areas in the United States – has remained as a home base for the world's rich and famous. The fate of many of the outlying areas such as Queen's and the Bronx, that joined the city in 1898, has not been so impressive. Was consolidation a factor? New York's municipal government is the largest in the United States. In 1975 it was to all intents and purposes bankrupt. Can these problems be traced in any way to consolidation? These questions are unlikely to be answered to anyone's satisfaction. But they should be kept in mind as we briefly review New York's consolidation saga.

The definitive account of the consolidation has been written by David C. Hammack, an historian at Columbia University. He divides the story into

12.Weigley, "The Border City," p.372.

two main periods. From 1887 to 1894, the consolidation movement was led by closely allied "mercantile, banking, real estate, and municipal reform elites." Weakened by internal divisions, the movement was then taken over by the New York state Republican party, which saw in consolidation a unique opportunity to advance its own interests.[13] Only when the political advantages became clear did state politicians make the necessary commitment. But without many years of groundwork, the political advantages would never have become apparent.

The movement for consolidation resulted from the fact that some business interests in New York were concerned that the city's economic growth did not appear to be keeping pace with that of more westerly cities, notably Chicago. Their most important belief was that "if a single municipal government could gain control over New York harbor and all the surrounding territory, it could promote the unified, comprehensive development of shipping, railroads, and related facilities in such a way as to aid both merchants and property owners."[14] In 1890, speaking to state legislators, one of consolidation's main proponents, Andrew H. Green, made a debatable claim of the kind that is frequently heard today. He argued that "New York was in competition with London, Paris, Chicago, and even Brooklyn... and all these had grown by increasing their boundaries; consolidation would enable the city to hold its own."[15]

In 1894 Green and his consolidationist colleagues convinced the legislature to conduct a referendum on the subject. Rather than explaining exactly what consolidation involved,

> ... Green had done everything he could to make the proposal so vague that every possible constituency could find something in it. In deference to the Chamber of Commerce and to his own sense of priorities, he had secured agreement from the legislature that Greater New York would include all the territory bordering on New York harbor. But he saw to it that other issues remained unresolved... Sampling opinion to determine where and how to pitch their message, they [consolidationists] sent speakers armed with different arguments into every corner of the metropolis.[16]

---

13. David C. Hammack, *Power and Society: Greater New York at the Turn of the Century* (New York: Russell Sage Foundation, 1982), pp.228-9.
14. Hammack, *Power and Society*, p.185.
15. Oliver E. Allen, *New York, New York* (New York: Athaneum, 1990), p.249.
16. Hammack, *Power and Society*, pp.204-5.

The greatest opposition came from the city of Brooklyn.[17] Anti-consolidationists there were concerned with identity, local control and, perhaps most of all, a fear that consolidation would cause New York's ethnic diversity to cross the East River and disrupt Brooklyn's stable and more typically American way of life. Pro-consolidationists coveted a share of Manhattan's tax base, which they assumed could be used to help lower Brooklyn's tax rates or provide better services. The problem, of course, was that open declarations of such benefits in Brooklyn stirred opposition to consolidation in Manhattan. In any event, the referendum carried in all the counties, but only by a vote of 64,744 to 64,467 in Brooklyn.[18]

The closeness of the vote mobilized the Brooklyn opposition – now organized as the League of Loyal Citizens – even more than before. Hammack summarizes one of its pamphlets in these words:

> Far from producing economical and efficient government... consolidation would prove to be expensive. New York City did have a low tax rate, but that would not last for long. New York had already launched several costly projects, and consolidation would serve Brooklyn's purposes only if more were added. But these projects would become hideously expensive because the monstrous size of the greater city would permit venal, slum-chosen public officials to operate hidden from the public eye.[19]

The situation in Brooklyn appeared to be spinning out of control and the consolidationist leaders, such as Andrew Green, could do little about it. This is when the state Republicans entered the picture. The tortured politics of the next three years are too complex to explore here. In essence, however, the Republicans decided that they had a chance of winning political control of a consolidated New York and that, in any event, there was much political credit to be gained by being seen as promoter of the city's apparent economic interests. The necessary legislation was approved in 1897 and on 1 January 1898 the new city of New York, with the same boundaries it has today, came into being.

The city's new charter contained few of the provisions favoured by many of the original proponents of consolidation, provisions that would have streamlined city institutions and made them less susceptible to takeover by the city's famous Democratic machine, Tammany Hall. Plans for reformed institutions in the new city had long since been eliminated because of the

---

17. See John Tierney, "Brooklyn Could Have Been a Contender," *The New York Times Magazine*, 28 December 1997, pp.18, 20-3, and 37-8.
18. Hammack, *Power and Society*, p.206.
19. Hammack, *Power and Society*, p.210.

need to ensure that Tammany politicians did not actively oppose consolidation. In any event, Tammany Hall narrowly won the first mayoral election, thus sabotaging one of the Republicans' main political objectives relating to consolidation.

The new charter maintained the constituent counties in place, defining them as boroughs for municipal government purposes. Voters in each borough elected a "borough president" to look after local concerns. In 1901, the borough presidents were given membership on the Board of Estimates, a kind of council executive committee, but in the 1980s, the U.S. Supreme Court ruled that this arrangement was unconstitutional because it violated their standards relating to one-man – one-vote.[20]

No one has ever argued that the New York consolidation saved money. Writing in 1942, Victor Jones reported that, "In the ten years following consolidation there was a sharp upward trend in expenditures and funded debt." Budget appropriations for the city increased from $78.4 million in 1898, to $98.6 million in 1903, and to $130.4 million in 1907. Between 1896 and 1899 tax rates in Manhattan went up by about 16 per cent, due largely to consolidation.[21] But, as Jones and others point out, the main purpose of the consolidation was to spend public money, not to save it. The figures that Jones reports should not be surprising. As a proponent of various forms of increased integration of municipal services across city-regions, Jones was quite frank in his overall conclusions about the implications for expenditures:

> The integration of local government in metropolitan areas may result, then, chiefly in an expansion, improvement, or equalization of services rather than in actual reductions of budget items. Some definite savings can be expected, however, from the integration of overhead administration. Even here, the most important result to the community will be the substitution of comprehensive for haphazard and competitive planning of services of metropolitan significance.[22]

Throughout the 20th century, the city of New York has been by far the most populous municipality in the United States. In 1996, with a population of 7.3 million, it was more than twice the size of its nearest rival, the city of Chicago. The city of New York's proportion of the total city-region population was also almost twice that of the city of Chicago (41 per cent vs

---

20. Allen, *New York, New York*, p.250.
21. *Metropolitan Government* (Chicago: University of Chicago Press, 1942), p.189.
22. *Metropolitan Government*, pp.199-200.

21 per cent).[23] Yet it was New York that was bankrupt in the mid-1970s, not Chicago. This is a puzzle that has been addressed by a number of analysts, including Paul E. Peterson, now a professor in the department of government at Harvard University.[24]

Peterson makes no reference to the consolidation of 1898. He does make extensive reference to the city's size and wealth. The essence of Peterson's analysis was that the city of New York was so big that it did not have to contend with the normal competitive pressures faced by every other municipality in the country. Peterson points out that, in 1974, New York's "per capita expenditures from local sources" (i.e. excluding expenditures financed from grants) were $578. The median figure for the next nine largest municipalities was $208. Part of the explanation for this difference is that New York was responsible for more governmental functions (even some hospitals and universities) than other municipalities. But this too is part of Peterson's case: because New York was so big, the state government expected it to do more. In any event, Peterson provides lots of evidence to show that even for common services provided by most municipal governments, New York's expenditures, wage levels, and per-capita number of employees were exceptionally high compared to those in other major American cities. He also shows that there was nothing distinctive about New York's spending levels in the 1960s and 1970s. Controlling for inflation, they had been growing at a constant annual rate of about four to five per cent since 1949.[25]

It is doubtless true that the city's expenditures have been better controlled since the virtual bankruptcy of the mid-1970s. The point, of course, is that the city obviously did not benefit from any possible economies of scale that resulted from its size. On the contrary, it appears that its size was one of the factors that caused the bankruptcy. It was the

---

23. Andrew Sancton, "Introduction" in Donald N. Rothblatt and Andrew Sancton, eds. *Metropolitan Governance Revisted* (Berkeley: Institute of Governmental Studies Press at the University of California, 1998), pp.2-3.

24. Peterson's book is *City Limits* (Chicago: University of Chicago Press, 1981). One of Peterson's students later wrote a more detailed and nuanced analysis explaining why New York went bankrupt and Chicago did not. See Ester R. Fuchs, *Mayors and money: Fiscal Policy in New York and Chicago* (Chicago: University of Chicago Press, 1992). Her explanation focuses on the continued existence within the city itself of the Democratic machine and of various, inde-pendent, special-purpose bodies. See also, Charles R. Morris, *The Cost of Good Intentions: New York City and the Liberal Experiment, 1960-1975* (New York: W. W. Norton, 1980).

25. *City Limits*, pp.198-206.

bankruptcy that caused New York's financial affairs to be put in order in the late 1970s and afterwards.

Notwithstanding New York's fiscal difficulties, it could be argued that the consolidated municipality was a crucial factor in maintaining and promoting the city's dominant position in the world economy. The problem with this argument is that none of the recent analysts of the phenomena of "world cities" even mention New York's municipal government, let alone the 1898 consolidation.[26] Perhaps such analysts, concerned as they are with corporate financing, information flows, and high technology, simply take municipal government for granted. It could be, however, that New York's physical infrastructure, as provided by its expensive consolidated municipal government, really is at the heart of its 20th-century success as the world's economic centre.

Consolidation did have an early impact on the city's infrastructure. In 1930, Paul Studenski stressed its importance in improving transportation and water supply systems, especially in areas of the city other than Manhattan. This, he claims, caused both industries and their workers to spread across the new city, leaving Manhattan free to become specialized in the commercial activities for which it became so well known. But Studenski, a supporter of the consolidation and of the general integration of municipalities in metropolitan areas, was also aware of the problems with consolidation.

> Various municipal services — streets, water, sewers — were extended into unimproved areas long in advance of any prospect of their development... This entailed waste. Sewers, for illustration, were laid... in the expectation that the cost would be met in large part by assessments for benefits. It frequently happened, however, that the speculative developers who originally requested the improvement were not the owners of the land subject to assessment at the time the assessment was levied... [T]he new owners... appealed for and obtained relief from the assessment. City police and other like services were provided in rural sections much in advance of reasonable need.[27]

In 1982, Michael N. Danielson and Jameson W. Doig, two professors at Princeton University, wrote an important book on the more recent development of New York's physical infrastructure. They were concerned

---

26. The literature here is huge. For a sample, see Paul L. Knox and Peter J. Taylor, eds. *World Cities in a World System* (Cambridge: Cambridge University Press, 1995).

27. *The Government of Metropolitan Areas*, p.363.

with demonstrating the extent to which "the actions of governmental organizations have a significant independent influence on urban development, rather than having no significant role, or affecting development only by ratifying and supporting decisions previously made in other subsystems of the society, such as the private marketplace."[28] Danielson and Doig wanted to counter claims by others that government was relatively unimportant for urban development. If ever there were to be a case that the government of the city of New York was important, this would be it. The authors point out, however, that in 1977 the city of New York was only one of 780 municipalities in what was defined by the Regional Plan Association as the New York Region. By mid-20th century its boundaries were far too limited for it to have any major impact on regional economic development.

Much of New York's transportation infrastructure has been developed by a remarkable network of special-purpose authorities. The most important of these authorities were the Triborough Bridge and Tunnel Authority (founded in 1933 and merged with the New York State Metropolitan Transportation Authority in 1967) and the Port Authority of New York and New Jersey (founded in 1921). The former was the main power base of Robert Moses, a man who never held any office within the city of New York but who is usually acknowledged as the main builder of much of the region's 20th-century transportation infrastructure.[29] The Transportation Authority controls the Long Island Rail Road, New York's subways, and some toll bridges. The Port Authority owns and operates the port facilities, bridges, airports (including JFK), a rail transit line, bus and truck terminals, and the World Trade Center.[30] The city of New York that resulted from the 1898 consolidation has many important municipal responsibilities, but providing the infrastructure for regional economic growth has not been one of them.

THE CONSOLIDATIONIST RETREAT

Nothing like New York's consolidation in 1898 has ever been seen again in the United States. For more than 100 years, no major city (such as

28.Michael N. Danielson and Jameson W. Doig, *New York: The Politics of Urban Regional Development* (Berkeley: University of California Press, 1982), p.1.
29.Robert A. Caro, *The Power Broker: Robert Moses and the Fall of New York* (New York: Alfred A. Knopf, 1974).
30.*New York*, p.5.

Brooklyn) has joined another. Since 1910,[31] no solvent American municipality has been forced against its will to lose its incorporated status and to join another. For the first few decades of this century, however, suburban municipalities in both the United States and Canada frequently joined central cities voluntarily. Such cities often could provide cheaper, better services that could be accessed only by areas that were included within their boundaries. In these circumstances, the incentives for amalgamation were obvious. Sometimes suburbs joined central cities to escape high debts and the resulting need for high tax levels.[32]

During this period the cities of Montreal and Toronto dramatically increased both their territories and their debts as a result of amalgamations with nearby suburbs. Indeed, today's municipal boundaries in Montreal can often be explained by amalgamations with the central city that did take place (Notre-Dame-de-Grâce) and ones that did not (Outremont, Westmount). Table 1 shows the territorial growth of the city of Montreal for the period 1883-1918. During this period the city's size increased from 6,299 acres to 32,458 acres.

TABLE 1: CITY OF MONTREAL'S TERRITORIAL GROWTH 1883 - 1918

DATE	MUNICIPALITY ANNEXED	ACRES
1883	Hochelaga	1,230
1886	Saint-Jean-Baptiste	308
1887	Saint-Gabriel	330
1893	Côte Saint-Louis	850
1905	Saint-Henri	450
1905	Sainte-Cunégonde	124
1906	Villeray	60
1906	Rosemont (part)	185
1906	Sault-au-Récollets (part)	836
1907	Saint-Laurent (part)	960

31. In 1901, a Colorado constitutional amendment, approved by state voters in a referendum, required six municipalities to join Denver. In 1907, the Pennsylvania legislature forced the city of Allegheny, against its will, to join Pittsburgh. In 1910, the Alabama legislature merged twelve municipalities with Birmingham after conducting a metropolitan-wide referendum by which the merger was approved by an overall majority, but not by a majority in the municipalities being merged. See Jon C. Teaford, *City and Suburb*, pp. 49-50, 74-75, and 86.
32. This process is well documented in Teaford, *City and Suburb*.

TABLE 1: CITY OF MONTREAL'S TERRITORIAL GROWTH 1883 - 1918

DATE	MUNICIPALITY ANNEXED	ACRES
1908	Notre-Dame-des-Neiges	1,131
1908	Rosemont (part)	249
1908	Sault-au-Récollets	314
1909	Delorimier	391
1909	Outremont (part)	17
1909	Saint-Louis	720
1910	Ahuntsic	727
1910	Bordeaux	868
1910	Beaurivage	46
1910	Ville-Émard	951
1910	Saint-Laurent (part)	877
1910	Notre-Dame-de-Grâce	2,536
1910	Côte-des-Neiges	1,420
1910	Saint-Paul	263
1910	Rosemont	1,432
1910	Tétraultville	311
1910	Longue-Pointe	4,194
1912	Côte-Saint-Luc (part)	373
1916	Saint-Laurent (part)	93
1916	Cartierville	1,293
1916	Sault-au-Récollets	1,150
1918	Saint-Laurent (part)	1
1918	Maisonneuve	1,157

SOURCE: Excerpt from a report of the Executive Committee of the city of Montreal, 1962, as reproduced in Quebec, Ministry of Municipal Affairs, *Study Commission of Intermunicipal Problems on the Island of Montreal* (Quebec: Queen's Printer, 1964), p.9. Jean-Pierre Collin reproduces this table (with some very slight differences and with an accompanying map) in "Les stratégies fiscales municipales et la gestion de l'agglomération urbaine: le cas de la ville de Montréal entre 1910-1965" in *Urban History Review – Revue d'histoire urbaine* 23-1 (November 1994) p.22. Professor Collin does not indicate the source of his table.

In the early 20th century, American suburban municipalities that did not need centre-city services, and rural ones that were relatively close to big cities, felt increasingly under threat. Consolidation in New York was seen by many as a dangerous precedent. More and more so-called experts – usually in the new academic fields of public administration and land-use planning – were claiming that state legislatures needed to impose some form of municipal integration in the country's largest city-regions.[33] The suburban defensive strategy was remarkably effective. Its main component involved amending state constitutions to limit the ability of state legislatures to impose boundary changes without local consent.

These provisions can be seen as taking three different forms, although they overlapped and were mutually reinforcing. In Canadian terms, we might say that the following items were "entrenched" within many state constitutions:

- **County boundaries and forms of government**, thereby preventing legislatures from disrupting county arrangements in order to facilitate the kinds of consolidations that occurred in Philadelphia and New York.

- **"Home rule,"** a series of constitutional provisions usually applying to larger municipalities stating that municipal boundaries and internal governmental arrangements could not be changed without the formal consent of the affected municipalities.

- **The prohibition of special legislation**, which meant that no laws could be approved that applied only to a specified municipality or group of municipalities and that all municipal legislation had to be general in its scope.

These provisions, and others like them, always leave lots of room for interpretation and evasion. Lawsuits resulting from them have been frequent. But they have meant that state legislatures have been prevented in the 20th century from imposing municipal consolidations, either because such action would obviously be unconstitutional or because it would provoke new constitutional amendments to make it unconstitutional.

In response, proponents of municipal consolidation launched various crusades to establish what they called "federative" metropolitan governments. Municipal boundaries would be left untouched but a new level of government would be established on top of them to cover the entire city-region. Until 1957, such crusades were fruitless. Consolidationists suffered one defeat after another. Municipal councils and voters – often in central cities as well as suburbs – refused to accept such new structures, causing still more claims that American city-regions had become

---

33. Paul Studenski and Victor Jones, whose work is previously cited in this chapter, are prime examples.

fragmented beyond hope, claims that would become even louder in the 1950s and 1960s.

CONCLUSION

Municipal boundaries were extremely fluid in late 19th and early 20th century North America. Suburban municipalities were easily created and many of them, mainly for financial reasons, soon decided to join the central city. This was a process in which state governments did little more than keep track of the paperwork. Sometimes legislation was required. The most dramatic examples of large-scale municipal amalgamations involving whole counties brought about by state legislation were Philadelphia in 1854 and New York in 1898. Even in these cases, however, there was considerable local support, manifested in New York by the referendum of 1894.

Since 1898, large-scale municipal amalgamations in major cities have not been part of the public agenda in the United States. Even most analysts who believe in the importance of increased contact between central cities and suburbs do not argue that consolidation is the solution. These more recent controversies will be examined in the chapter after next. In the intervening chapter, we shall leave the U.S. to examine what happened in other countries during the 1960s and 1970s, a period during which there was a remarkable belief that, by improving the structural organizations of government, we could improve the societies that they were supposed to be serving.

CHAPTER 2

THE ERA OF BIG GOVERNMENT: THE 1960s AND 1970s

T hroughout the first half of the 20th century there was no shortage of proposals to reorganize urban governments in liberal democracies. In the real world, however, not much happened. Politicians had other things on their minds, notably two world wars and the Great Depression of the 1930s. The latter had a profound impact on local governments. They were shown to be quite incapable of supporting massive numbers of unemployed and, in most jurisdictions, they eventually surrendered financial responsibility for this function to senior governments. Many municipal governments in North America were effectively bankrupted by borrowing funds for new infrastructure in the 1920s on the false assumption that new development would pay for it in the 1930s. This experience was the origin of tighter central controls on local borrowing and of the fiscal conservatism that remains a characteristic of many municipal governments even to this day.[1] The Depression also demonstrated to many that dramatic government intervention to fix social and economic problems was both possible and, in many cases at least, even necessary. Following World War II and after the subsequent boom period of reconstruction and economic renewal subsided, it was not surprising that many looked to government for solutions.

Part of this government-centred search for solutions involved the so-called "modernization" of local government. Small municipal governments – especially those in urban areas – seemed hopelessly out of touch with the spirit of the times. Since there was great faith in what central governments

---

1. In Windsor, Ontario, the province's solution to imminent municipal bankruptcy in 1935 was to impose a merger of four municipalities, including Walkerville whose strong tax base was used to help rescue the others. See Larry Kulisek and Trevor Price, "Ontario Municipal Policy Affecting Local Autonomy: A Case Study Involving Windsor and Toronto," *Urban History Review*, 16-3 (February 1988), 255-70.

could do, there was little opposition – outside the United States at least – to the notion that they could effectively reorganize long-standing arrangements for local government so that it would not be left behind by the wonders of technological progress. For example, computers were of great potential use in storing municipal data, billing for utilities and taxes, and helping to project demand for new services and facilities. But they were so expensive that only the largest of municipalities could possibly afford them. Enabling all police in the territory of the Montreal Urban Community (MUC) to have access to central computer facilities was a significant reason for creating the unified MUC police department in 1972.

This chapter is about how different central governments in liberal democracies responded to pressures for local reorganization. The story begins in Britain in the late 1950s when a royal commission was examining local government in London. Its work resulted in the amalgamation of groups of London boroughs and in the creation of the Greater London Council. Later in the 1960s another royal commission investigated local government in the rest of England. The subsequent debate and legislation are profoundly important to any understanding of the current controversies relating to municipal amalgamation. Events in Britain affected municipal reorganization in Ontario, first in Toronto and then in other urban areas in Ontario. In 1965 the City of Laval was created in Quebec, the most significant legislated municipal merger in North America since New York in 1898. Four years later it was eclipsed by the NDP-sponsored legislation in Winnipeg that established a "Unicity" where there had previously been a metropolitan authority and 13 constituent municipalities. The last section of the chapter briefly examines other countries in which major amalgamations took place – Denmark, Sweden, and Germany – and even more briefly at those where they did not – France, Italy, and Greece.

GREAT BRITAIN

The municipal corporations that govern Britain's cities have their roots deep in the Middle Ages. The network of special-purpose bodies and rural authorities that grew up around them was incredibly complex. It was not until the 19th century that the British Parliament brought some order to the system by establishing most urban municipal corporations as single-tier "county boroughs" and by creating a two-tier county system covering rural areas, towns, and villages. It was this same system that was established in the Province of Canada (now Quebec and Ontario) in the mid-19th century.

Prior to 1888, the London city-region was governed by a tiny city of London (which still exists today and is best known as "the City," the location for London's thriving financial-services activities), a powerful Metropolitan Board of Works, and hundreds of other local authorities of various kinds. Parliament established the London County Council (LCC) in 1888, a directly elected body superimposed on existing authorities. It was given no authority over "the City." In 1899, all local authorities within the jurisdiction of the LCC were reorganized into 28 "metropolitan boroughs."[2]

This system remained in place until 1964. The changes that came into effect that year were a direct response to the *Report of the Royal Commission on Local Government in Greater London, 1957-60*, also known as the Herbert Report after its chair, Sir Edwin Herbert. The fundamental problem that faced the royal commission was that London had grown far beyond the boundaries of the LCC. However, this issue will not be considered here because no one proposed that all the built-up area should be merged into one single-tier municipality. For the purposes of this report, what is of interest in the work of the Herbert commission is its approach to the issue of the size and functions of lower-tier authorities within metropolitan federations.

The Herbert commission recommended the establishment of a Greater London Council (GLC) covering a much wider territory than the old LCC. It also recommended that there be 52 constituent "Greater London Boroughs," with a minimum population of 100,000 each. This involved only limited disruption of the existing metropolitan boroughs within the LCC and of the larger county boroughs and lower-tier units outside the LCC. But when the government published its White Paper on the issue in 1961, it reduced the number of boroughs by setting the minimum population at 200,000. The reason for this was that contrary to the Herbert recommendations, the government wanted education to remain a borough responsibility (at least outside the area of the old LCC) and it decided that for education purposes, London's local authorities had to be significantly larger than 100,000 in population. After much controversy about various particular amalgamations, the end result was that the GLC contained 32 boroughs, each with its own mayor and council. These municipalities –

---

2. The history of local government in London is very well documented. The account here relies on the following two works: Frank Smallwood, *Greater London: The Politics of Metropolitan Reform* (Indianapolis: Bobbs-Merrill, 1965) and Gerald Rhodes, *The Government of London: The Struggle for Reform* (Toronto: University of Toronto Press, 1970).

together with the city of London – still exist today, with the same boundaries that came into being in 1964. The GLC does not.

Much of the debate about exactly which lower-tier units were to be merged with each other revolved around the search for partisan political advantage. Conservatives held office nationally; Labour controlled the LCC and most of its boroughs. Almost all issues relating to boundaries were viewed through the lenses of party politics. But the issue of the minimum size of boroughs related to what can best be labelled "functional" considerations. The function most in dispute was education. To place it under the control of the GLC was to remove it too far from local community control. To place it under split jurisdiction of the GLC and relatively small boroughs was seen by educational administrators and teachers as a recipe for disaster. The solution was to make the boroughs bigger. Had education – and possibly social services such as child protection – not been a functional responsibility of British municipal authorities, then much of the pressure for larger lower-tier units in London would have been absent.

In 1968 the Labour government appointed a royal commission, chaired by Lord Redcliffe-Maud, to make recommendations concerning local government in the rest of England. The most pressing concern seemed to be that large cities – county boroughs – were totally removed from the two-tier systems of local government that covered their rural hinterlands. There were two possible solutions to the perceived problem: extend the county boroughs out into the countryside, thereby creating a single-tier system, or bring the county boroughs within the jurisdiction of the counties. A majority in the commission recommended the former; one dissenting member recommended the latter. But the Conservative government that took office in 1970 chose the two-tier option, but with different boundaries from what the dissenting opinion recommended. All of the various options involved a drastic reduction in the number of English municipalities.

The work of the Redcliffe-Maud commission is significant in many ways, one of which was that it sponsored research relating to the relationship between local government size and efficiency for various local government functions. Its own statistical research did not demonstrate that services provided by existing larger local governments were more efficiently provided than by existing smaller ones.[3] How the royal commission dealt with the findings of its own commissioned research makes for fascinating reading and will therefore be quoted at some length:

3. United Kingdom, Royal Commission on Local Government in England, *Econo-mies of Scale in Local Government Services*, Research Study 3, Cmnd. 4040-II (London: Her Majesty's Stationary Office, 1969).

The over-riding impression which emerges from the three studies by outside bodies and from our own study of staffing is that size cannot statistically be proved to have a very important effect on performance. There were a few scattered instances where economies of scale seemed to be operating, for example in larger counties and county boroughs in relation to highways...

An... important problem is that of finding a satisfactory measure of performance. All three of the studies undertaken for us by outside bodies try to solve this problem, by one means or another; but it remains very hard indeed to quantify the various facets of each service or to distinguish 'good' from 'barely adequate' or 'bad.' We realise, too, that 'quality' of service cannot be isolated from the environment in which the service is provided. Local authorities vary enormously in their problems and the conditions in which they have to work. The studies attempted to take this into account, but very serious problems of measurement remained.[4]

Here the royal commission is saying that it is profoundly suspicious of the findings of its own research studies. Because of these suspicions, it then asked central government departments to assess the relationship between size and performance. Here are its comments on what the central departments had to say:

...the two studies by central departments were particularly helpful since they enabled us to supplement what were essentially statistical exercises with the *subjective* [my emphasis] impressions of those who have direct, disinterested knowledge of the quality of local authority performance in two major services. They both showed that size was related to performance. From returns made to Your Majesty's Inspectorate, the Department of Education and Science concluded that the least efficient educational authorities tended to have populations below the 200,000 mark and that authorities above 200,000, but less than 500,000 provided an acceptable or better education service. The best average performance came from authorities with populations above 500,000. The study by the Home Office found a rather less positive correlation between size and efficiency. Nevertheless, the general trends were clear: the most efficient children's service was provided by authorities with populations between 350,000 and 500,000 and those providing the least efficient service tended to have populations below 200,000.[5]

4. United Kingdom, Royal Commission on Local Government in England, *Report*, Cmnd. 4040 (London: Her Majesty's Stationary Office, 1969), p58.
5. United Kingdom, *Report* (Cmnd 4040) 1969, pp.58-9.

45

These passages – in which statistical evidence is deftly brushed aside and replaced by the impressions of central government inspectors – are now legendary among students of British local government. One of them, John Dearlove, has succinctly captured the commissioners' dilemma when they realized that their preconceived notions about the benefits of increased size did not match the facts:

> There were only two options. They could accept the evidence of the outside research studies, cast the orthodox rule of reform to the wind, operate outside the framework and assumptions of the conventional wisdom, and devise some alternative formula to guide the course of their reorganising endeavours. Alternatively, they could stand by the orthodoxy, in which case they would need to discredit the research studies and find some alternative base from which to legitimise their approach to reorganisation. It was a fight between fact and preconceived commitment and "knowledge." There was no contest: the widely shared and long-established rule of reform was seen as right, and the facts were wrong.[6]

In any event, as a result of legislated local government reorganization throughout the United Kingdom between 1960 and 1975, the total number of municipalities was reduced from 1,349 to 521.[7]

METROPOLITAN TORONTO AND ONTARIO'S REGIONAL GOVERNMENTS

In 1953 the Municipality of Metropolitan Toronto (Metro) came into being as North America's first upper-tier multi-functional urban government. The lower-tier constituent units of this metropolitan federation were 13 existing municipalities: the city of Toronto, four towns, three villages, and five townships. For many years to come Toronto's metro system would be much admired and studied throughout the world as a model of

---

6. John Dearlove, *The Reorganisation of British Local Government: Old Orthodoxies and a Political Perspective* (London: Cambridge University Press, 1979), p.71.
7. L.J. Sharpe, "Local Government Reorganization: General Theory and UK Practice" in Bruno Dente and Francesco Kjellberg, eds. *The Dynamics of Institutional Change: Local Government Reorganization in Western Democracies* (London: SAGE, 1988), p.99.

governmental arrangements for city-regions. By all accounts[8] it was an outstanding success, using the city's lucrative tax base to fund infrastructure development in the far-flung urbanizing townships of Etobicoke, North York, and Scarborough.

In 1963, the Ontario government appointed Carl Goldenberg of Montreal as a one-man royal commission to report on various matters relating to Metro's structure and organization. The most pressing problems involved political representation. Under the original system, the city was given 13 representatives with one vote each on Metro council and each of the heads of council of the 13 other municipalities was given one vote. But by 1963, the city's population was only 38.1 per cent of Metro's total population. The reeve of North York had one vote on Metro council representing 308,000 people and so did the reeve of Swansea, representing 9000.[9]

As it did in the early 1950s, the city of Toronto advocated total amalgamation. It argued that "an outright merger is the simplest and most logical governmental arrangement, offering the best prospects for continuing achievement."[10] Mr. Goldenberg's response was that "'neat and tidy' solutions to complex problems of government are not necessarily applicable or practical" and that "such savings in costs as may be effected would soon be more than offset by the increase in expenditures to raise the standards of services to a common level."[11]

Mr. Goldenberg recommended that the 13 units be consolidated into four. He explained his approach in these words:

> My recommendations for a consolidation of area municipalities are not based on theories as to the "optimum" size of a municipality in terms of population. Much has been written on this subject and the briefs to the Commission made many references to such writings, but there is no agreement as to the "optimum," and the figures vary widely with the criteria applied. I agree with the Royal Commission on Greater London [Herbert commission] that "there is no special value in any one figure." In fact, it cannot be said that there is one optimum size for municipalities. What may be the appropriate size of constituent units of one metropolitan area will not necessarily be appropriate to another with different characteristics

8. The major books are Albert Rose, *Governing Metropolitan Toronto: A Social and Political Analysis, 1953-1971* (Berkeley: University of California Press, 1972) and Timothy J. Colton, *Big Daddy: Frederick G. Gardiner and the Building of Metropolitan Toronto* (Toronto: University of Toronto Press, 1980).
9. Ontario, *Report of the Royal Commission on Metropolitan Toronto* (1965), p.1.
10. City of Toronto's brief as quoted in Ontario, *Report* (1965), p.176.
11. Ontario, *Report* (1965), pp.176 & 177.

derived from its own history, geography, population, composition, and economic development.[12]

Having written this, Mr. Goldenberg went on to recommend that the 13 constituent municipalities be consolidated into four. In particular, he called for five inner suburbs to be joined with the city of Toronto. His main justifications for this were that they

> ...are linked by geography and common interests. They are mature and developed areas... With each municipality seeking to improve its tax base independently, they compete for development and redevelopment projects, which are accordingly dealt with on a piecemeal basis and without regard to sound planning in the overall interests of the area.

> The six municipalities are highly interdependent.

> A look at the map shows the highly artificial boundaries which separate each of the five suburbs from the City of Toronto. Each is a political unit, but in terms of geography and of social and economic interdependence they are all parts of the City. It is only logical that they should be merged with it politically. A consolidation of the five suburbs with the City of Toronto will strengthen the core upon which the strength of the Metropolitan Area as a whole depends. It will make possible the coordination of planning for urban renewal and redevelopment by one planning body operating under one local council. It will also eliminate the unfair disparities in financial burdens and inequalities in the range and standard of services in the area of the 54 square miles covered by the six municipalities.[13]

This is a classic statement of the consolidationist position, except that there is no reference to saving money.

The problem with Goldenberg's position was that his decision as to what to include within the city was quite arbitrary. Although he referred to "artificial boundaries," he was quite content to leave the southern boundary of North York in place as the boundary between North York and the expanded city of Toronto. It was just as "arbitrary" as any border he wanted to abolish. Everything that he wrote about the five "inner suburbs" applied equally to much of southern North York. Indeed, the arbitrariness of it all became especially apparent in 1966 when the Robarts government announced that the provincial government was accepting most of Goldenberg's recommendations, but not his preference that there be four cities within Metro. The government said there would be one city of Toronto

12. Ontario, *Report*, (1965) p.180.
13. Ontario, *Report* (1965), pp.181-2.

and five "boroughs." Only two municipalities (Swansea and Forest Hill) would be joined to the city (increasing its 1963 population from 630,000 to 660,000),[14] not five as Goldenberg had recommended. Premier Robarts gave no reason for adopting a different position.[15] The new arrangements for Metro were effective on 1 January 1967. Until all six of Metro's constituent municipalities were merged on 1 January 1998, their boundaries were never again changed.

From the late-1960s until the mid-1970s, the Ontario government conducted a vigorous campaign to reorganize municipal arrangements in most of Ontario's urban areas. This led to one stand-alone merger: Port Arthur and Fort William to form Thunder Bay in 1970, a rather special case because the two municipalities were "twin cities" in an isolated part of the province.[16] Better known is Ontario's creation of 11 two-tier systems of regional government. The bringing together of urban and rural in new upper-tier councils caused considerable political difficulty, but that is not what concerns us here. More relevant to this report is that, as part of the reorganization inherent in all the new regional governments, there were many lower-tier consolidations. It was as though the 1967 changes in municipal boundaries within Metro Toronto had been made at the same time as it was first established in 1953.

Most of the amalgamations that were part of the process of creating regional governments involved the merger of rural townships and of cities, towns, and villages with such townships. There were no examples of cities being forced to merge with each other and only a very few in which towns were merged. After all the regional reorganizations were in place, the adjoining cities of Kitchener and Waterloo still existed. Eastview (later the city of Vanier) and the village of Rockcliffe Park were still in place even though they were contiguous with the city of Ottawa; so were the contiguous towns of Oakville and Durlington in Halton Region, and Stonoy Creek and Dundas, both adjoining the city of Hamilton.

Within Peel region, the towns of Port Credit and Streetsville were joined with Toronto township to create the city of Mississauga, and within Halton the towns of Georgetown and Acton were merged with much of Esquesing township to create the town of Halton Hills. But the best known lower-tier

14. Ontario, *Report* (1965), p.1.
15. Ontario, "Statement by the Honourable John Robarts, Prime Minister of Ontario, Re Report of the Royal Commission on Metropolitan Toronto,"10 January, 1966, pp.11-12.
16. Ontario, Ministry of Municipal Affairs, Lakehead Local Government Review, *Report and Recommendations* (1968).

amalgamation was within Waterloo region. When that region came into being in 1973, the city of Galt and the towns of Preston and Hespeler were amalgamated to form the new city of Cambridge. In a 186-page study in 1970 that led to the region's creation, Professor Stewart Fyfe of Queen's University devoted one paragraph to justifying the proposed merger:

> The case for amalgamating Galt, Preston, and Hespeler is strong. They are growing together physically and have many problems and some services in common. Both Hespeler and Preston are faced with the probability of considerable development once immediate servicing problems are overcome. It would seem best that these be solved on a common basis, particularly as the financial and administrative resources of Preston and Hespeler are necessarily limited and the impact of these developments upon Galt are inevitable and considerable.[17]

Since Professor Fyfe recommended this merger even if the government established an upper-tier regional authority responsible for sewers, water supply, and main roads, it is not at all clear what the merger was supposed to accomplish. It certainly was not designed to reduce costs:

> Some net increase is inevitable because one of the grounds for reorganization is to improve quality of services and reduce financial inequities. This means spending more money. It is sometimes referred to as the "levelling up" effect, meaning that when municipalities are combined, one does not bring all services to a common level, which while only improving quality of services for some might reduce it for others. Rather, the pressure is to raise the level of services up to what is considered the best level.[18]

There are two interesting postscripts to the Cambridge story. In a 1978 referendum, voters in Cambridge chose to secede from the region. In 1979, another provincial review commission addressed this issue and many others relating to the region's operation. The commissioner, W.H. Palmer, presented considerable data to show that Cambridge was better off within the region than outside it. Part of his argument relied on measurement of travel flows:

> Much of the concern about a lack of community between Kitchener and Cambridge originates from the Galt portion of the city. In fact, there is substantial vehicle traffic which originates in Galt and travels to Kitchener

---

17. Ontario, Ministry of Municipal Affairs, Waterloo Area Local Government Review, *Report* (1970), p.179.
18. Ontario, *Report* (1970), pp.169-70.

each day... [W]hile the largest single destination for Galt traffic is Kitchener-Waterloo, on a per capita basis the K-W area is 3.13 times as important to Preston and 3.68 times as important to Hespeler as it is to Galt.[19]

If such figures are relevant to debates about the organization of municipalities – and this is highly questionable – then surely they point to the inappropriateness of the merger in the first place.

The second postscript is that, in 1999, Cambridge city council finds itself as one of the main opponents of current proposals to merge all the constituent municipalities of Waterloo region into one. Long-time residents of the areas that were once Galt, Preston, or Hespeler must wonder if the process of forced municipal amalgamation can ever arrive at a natural conclusion. Guelph and Brantford are not far away.

LAVAL, QUEBEC[20]

Within Canada, Ontario was the most active province in municipal reorganization in the 1960s. On the advice of Carl Goldenberg, New Brunswick merged the city of Lancaster with the city of Saint John in 1967. But the most comprehensive single merger in North America since New York in 1898 took place in 1965 on Ile-Jésus, just north of Montreal, when 14 municipalities were merged to form the new city of Laval, Quebec's second most populous municipality.

Despite its obvious importance and the fact that it happened almost 35 years ago, the Laval amalgamation has received virtually no academic

---

19. Ontario, Ministry of Intergovernmental Affairs, *Report of the Waterloo Region Review Commission* (1979), p.99.
20. The material in this section is an abridged version of chapter 2 of a report written by Andrew Sancton, Rebecca James, and Rick Ramsay entitled *Amalgamation vs. Inter-municipal Co-operation: Financing Local and Infrastructure Costs* scheduled to be published by the Intergovernmental Committee on Urban and Regional Research (ICURR). Financial assistance from ICURR in conducting this research is gratefully acknowledged. I have also greatly benefitted from work by Nathaly Raynault. Ms. Raynault completed her MPA research project on the Laval amalgamation at the University of Western Ontario in 1999.

attention.[21] Nor has the government of Quebec sponsored any kind of systematic evaluation or study. Since claims are often made that the benefits of municipal amalgamation only become evident in the long term,[22] the Laval case is especially deserving of further study.

Between 1951 and 1964 the population of the territory of the 14 municipalities grew from 35,000 to 170,000[23]. The area, almost all of which is contained on a single island, was in the direct path of Montreal's outward suburban expansion. The creation of Laval – unlike that of Winnipeg's Unicity a few years later – had nothing to do with linking a central city with its suburban hinterland. Because Laval was and is a *suburban* amalgamation, it must be assessed not just in terms of how it affected the residents of its constituent municipalities but also in relation to its impact on the entire Montreal metropolitan area.

In 1964 the Quebec government established the Sylvestre Commission to study inter-municipal problems on Ile-Jésus. Its 248-page report is a remarkable document. It contains all the standard arguments for and against municipal amalgamation, as well as a few of its own. More so than with any other Canadian amalgamation debate, the one on Ile-Jésus seemed concerned with the evil effects of land speculation. The commission devoted eight pages[24] to its own analysis of the problem, but it never demonstrated how changes in municipal structures could reduce speculation. Instead, it recommended that a separate law be passed to prevent land speculation.[25] The commission implicitly assumed that larger municipalities are more effective land-use planners and that such planning reduces speculation, but the case was never clearly articulated.

In summary, the commission found an imposing list of weaknesses concerning municipal government on Ile-Jésus:

...déséquilibre de l'assiette foncière du aux modalités de développement, déficits accumulés, proportions alarmantes de la dette, mauvaise

---

21. A recent exception is the work of Jacques Desbiens, professor of public administration at l'Université du Québec à Chicoutimi. For his comments on Laval, see Luc Chartrand, "Villes: fusions attention!" *l'Actualité* 11 November 1999, pp.19-20.
22. Allan O'Brien, *Municipal Consolidation in Canada and its Alternatives* (Toronto: ICURR Press, 1993), p.110.
23. Jean Meynaud and Jacques Léveillée, *La régionalisation municipale au Québec* (Montreal: Editions Nouvelle Frontière, 1973), p.202.
24. Quebec, Ministère des affaires municipales, Commission d'étude sur les problèmes intermunicipaux de l'Ile Jésus, *Rapport final* (1964), pp.148-56.
25. Quebec, *Rapport final* (1964), p.254.

> utilisation des ressources humaines et matérielles, frictions politiques, manque de coordination et de continuité dans l'esprit et dans l'action, l'inexistence et abandon de certaines fonctions, performance incomplète et inadéquate des fonctions.[26]

It outlined the need for a single authority to capture economies of scale, to make sure that everyone shares the full costs of services they consume, and to make possible island-wide planning. It specifically rejected the establishment of a "supramunicipal" authority imposed on top of the existing municipalities. It pointed to the negative lessons that were to be learned from *Corporation Interurbaine de l'Ile Jésus*, the Montreal Metropolitan Corporation, the Municipality of Metropolitan Toronto, and similar authorities elsewhere.[27]

The commission's final recommendations are quite confusing. It carefully builds a case for a municipal system made up of six distinct "unités ou zones administratives" to be included within a supramunicipal authority, the governing body of which would be composed of members elected at large throughout the entire island. Local councils of the six units would be elected by wards.[28] Then it reverses direction and claims that this is a "solution d'avenir" that cannot be implemented immediately. Action on island-wide problems is urgent. But the populations of the six proposed units are far from equal and citizens would have difficulty grasping the complexities of the ideal system. Therefore, in the immediate future, there should be "Une Ville Unique dans l'Ile Jésus"[29] to be called "Laval."

> La commission s'oppose au gigantisme. Il est difficile de prévoir quand la Cité de Laval aura atteint cette limite de la ville géante. Tout indique, cependant, qu'elle devra y parvenir et c'est pourquoi la commission accepte, en principe, cette formation future d'un Gouvernement Supramunicipal entourés d'unités bien équilibrées devant jouir d'un statut d'autogestion.[30]

In short, the Sylvestre commission proposed that Laval should evolve in exactly the opposite way to what eventually happened in Metro Toronto. Laval should be unified first and converted to a two-tier system at some point in the future.

---

26. Quebec, *Rapport final* (1964), p.181.
27. Quebec, *Rapport final* (1964), p.187.
28. Quebec, *Rapport final* (1964), p.194.
29. Quebec, *Rapport final* (1964), p.200.
30. Quebec, *Rapport final* (1964), pp.251-2.

Six months later, the minister of municipal affairs, Pierre Laporte, presented legislation to create Laval, claiming there would be 500,000 people living on Ile-Jésus by 1981.[31] His justification for the amalgamation followed closely that of the Sylvestre report, although he was not convinced that the new city should later be dismantled and replaced by a two-tier system. Debate was rancorous. The *Union nationale* was strongly opposed. Speaking during third reading, its leader, Daniel Johnson, stated:

> [S]i le bill était accompagné de clauses empêchant la spéculation sur l'Ile-Jésus, si cette loi contenait les précautions nécessaires pour que le nouveau conseil ne dirige pas le développement dans le sens des intérêts dans lesquels eux ont une participation dans bien des cas, participation avouée publiquement par certains maires dont le député de Chomedey, je serais peut-être en faveur du bill. Mais sans cette clause contre la spéculation, jamais je ne me ferai le complice d'un pareil coup de force, d'un pareil assaut contre la démocratie.[32]

Notwithstanding the opposition's various delaying tactics, the bill was approved in August 1965. The first elections for Laval's city council were held in November.

The Laval amalgamation is now more almost 35 years old. A few points are obvious. First, contrary to recommendations in the Sylvestre report, there has been no serious talk of de-amalgamation. Perhaps this is because the population projections that the Sylvestre commission was working with turned out to be spectacularly wrong. Instead of 500,000 people in 1981, the actual population turned out to be only about 265,000. Given that the population in 1966 was already 196,000, Laval's growth rate would have had to have been three times greater between 1966 and 1981 to reach the 1981 projected figure! Even by 1996 the population total was only 330,000. But such miscalculations say little about the peculiarities of development in Laval, and nothing about the effects of amalgamation. They relate much more to the wildly optimistic spirit of the mid-1960s. *Horizon 2000*, the City of Montreal's 1967 attempt at a planning document for the whole city-region, projected population for the entire metropolitan area in 2000 to be seven million.[33] The actual figure for 1996 was just less than half that number.

31. Quebec, l'Assemblée legislative, *Débats*, 1965, p.4128.
32. Quebec, *Débats*, 1965, p.4573.
33. Jean-Claude Marsan, *Montreal in Evolution: Historical Analysis of the Development of Montreal's Architecture and Urban Environment* (Montreal: McGill-Queen's University Press, 1981), p.332.

Whether Laval is "better planned" than it would have been without amalgamation is exceptionally difficult to judge. An outsider might be impressed that much of Laval, especially in the north and northeast, contains relatively unspoiled agricultural land that is largely devoid of the haphazard strip development often found in an unregulated urban/rural fringe. But this could have more to do with slow growth than with good planning. More likely, it reflects the impact of *provincial* land-use policies, in particular the effects of the *Agricultural Land Preservation Act*, introduced by the *Parti québécois* government in 1978. The passage of this legislation went a long way to meet the Sylvestre commission's call for powerful policies to prevent land speculation. Regulations under the act establish permanent agricultural zones in Laval and in all other municipalities containing agricultural land. The zones would have existed whether Laval had been created or not – but this is something the Syvlestre commission and the Liberal government in the 1960s could not have known.

Determining whether or not the Laval amalgamation has saved any money is extremely difficult because we have no idea what costs would have been in the absence of amalgamation. Luckily, however, much of the "south shore" area of Montreal across the St. Lawrence River from downtown developed at the same time as Laval and in roughly the same way. In 1965-66 the 14 municipalities on Ile-Jésus had a total population of 196,088. Their total municipal expenditures were $20,150,955. Nine municipalities covering the territory of what is now the *Municipalité régionale de comté* (MRC) *de Champlain* had a population of 160,626 and spent $14,986,152.[34] Per capita municipal spending was $103 and $93 respectively in the two groups of municipalities. By 1996 per capita spending in Laval (1996 population of 330,393) had increased to $1,243 and in the (now) six municipalities of MRC Champlain (1996 population of 314,306) to $971.[35] In the 30-year period since Laval's creation, the amount by which municipal spending was higher in Laval than in the south shore increased from 10.7 per cent to 21.9 per cent. Such numbers tell us nothing about levels of service – but they do suggest that amalgamation

---

34. Expenditure data from Quebec, Ministère de l'Industrie et du Commerce, Bureau de la statistique du Québec, *Finances municipales pour l'année ter-minée le 30 avril 1966* (1966), pp.155, 161, and 165. Data for MRC Champlain municipalities exclude Préville, which became part of Saint-Lambert in 1966. Its 1966 population was 1299, but no financial information is available.

35. Expenditure data come from Quebec, Ministère des affaires municipales, *Finances des organismes municipaux pour l'exercice financier 1996* (Quebec: les Publications du Québec, 1998), pp.B-51 and B-55. All population data in this section are from the relevant federal census.

does not invariably lead to lower spending levels. In fact, they suggest the opposite.

On the basis of the Sylvestre report, one might have expected Laval to have invested more in environmental infrastructure. Comparing Laval and the south shore in this regard is not easy, because it would be very difficult to document the exact state of the infrastructure as it existed in the mid-1960s. Nevertheless, it is instructive to note that both areas were very slow to build major primary sewage treatment plants. The south-shore area plant did not open until 1992. It was a joint project of all the municipalities within MRC Champlain as well as the Town of Boucherville. The plant is managed by the City of Longueuil. In Laval, a similar plant has recently been constructed. In both cases the Government of Quebec absorbed 90 per cent of the cost. One reason for the delay in Laval was that officials in the neighbouring Montreal Urban Community believed Laval could be served more efficiently by its under-used plant at the east end of the Island of Montreal. Until Laval convinced the provincial government otherwise, it could not proceed. Once again, this comparison perhaps proves little – except that amalgamation does not guarantee infrastructure investment and fragmentation does not prevent it.

There remains one important way in which the creation of an amalgamated Laval might have made a difference. Readers of Canada's business press probably know much more about Laval than they do about any municipality in MRC Champlain. This is because in recent years Laval has agressively marketed itself as "Laval Technopole," a hospitable location for new investment of all kinds, especially biomedical industries and agribusiness. Laval even has its own *Parc scientifique et de haute technologie*, nestled among trees and greenery just west of the Laurentian Autoroute. Most of the occupants are pharmaceutical companies. In its northern (undeveloped) part, the park actually straddles the old border between Laval-des-Rapides and Chomedey, suggesting that without amalgamation, the park would not exist, at least not on the grand scale it does now.

Since the mid-1960s one of the great concerns about Montreal has been the loss of employment opportunities in the central part of the Island of Montreal and the general dispersion of economic activity off the island to the north and south. Although it is unlikely that the creation of Laval had much to do with either starting or strengthening this process, the city of Laval, Quebec's second most populous municipality, is a powerful presence in the metropolitan political arena. Was there ever an advantage to Quebec as a whole, and the Greater Montreal area in particular, in having one suburban municipality that is so large? Had Laval never been created, the subsequent development of arrangements for metropolitan governance in Montreal might well have taken a quite different turn, one that might have made it easier to establish co-ordinating institutions for local government that covered the entire city-region.

WINNIPEG[36]

Like the creation of Thunder Bay in 1970, the amalgamation in Winnipeg in 1972 was a deliberate effort to establish a single municipality for an entire city-region. It was therefore something quite different from the amalgamations that accompanied the creation of new two-tier systems in Britain and Ontario and from the suburban amalgamation in Laval. In the early 1970s there were other major cities in Canada – notably Calgary, Saskatoon, Regina, and London, Ontario – that covered almost all of their city-regions' built-up areas, but these other cities had expanded in modern times by absorbing parts of surrounding rural municipalities rather than being merged by provincial legislation with suburban cities, towns, and villages. This discussion about Winnipeg is therefore not just about a municipal amalgamation. It is about a method of governing an entire city-region.

Winnipeg's comprehensive one-tier system, known as "Unicity," came into effect on 1 January 1972. It replaced a two-tier system comprising a Metropolitan Corporation of Greater Winnipeg and 12 lower-tier municipalities. Although introduced by the New Democratic Party [NDP] government led by Ed Schreyer, total amalgamation had long been an objective of central-city business interests convinced that "governmental fragmentation was hurting development."[37] The NDP *White Paper on Unicity* echoed such concerns. After noting that "more than half the people in the entire province live in the Greater Winnipeg area" and that "the greater part of all goods and services produced in the province are generated in this area," the White Paper then claimed that the area has

36. This is a revised an updated version of the discussion of Winnipeg found in Andrew Sancton, *Governing Canada's City-Regions* (Montreal: Institute for Research on Public Policy, 1994), pp.22-8.
37. Meyer Brownstone and T.J. Plunkett, *Metropolitan Winnipeg: Politics and Reform of Local Government* (Berkeley: University of California Press, 1983), p. 30.

also "become the greatest single repository of social ills within the province."[38]

The authors of the White Paper discerned a direct link between the city's problems and its structures of government:

> The lines of authority in many instances were blurred, or else duplicated. Individual citizens and development investors alike became confused and often exasperated in any attempt to unravel the complex lines of authority. And, overlaid on the inherent confusions of a two-tier system... was, and is, the simple fact that the problems and difficulties of the urban community transcend jurisdictions and boundary lines. Yet the effective power to deal with these problems has been, and is, sharply delineated and circumscribed...[39]

The rest of the White Paper outlines new structures aimed at promoting economic growth, administrative efficiency, area-wide equity in levels of municipal services and property taxes, and greater opportunities for citizen participation through what were called community committees and residents' advisory groups.

After Unicity's creation, most of the attention focused on the new structures. Was a council of 51 members too large? Should the mayor be directly elected? What were the community committees really supposed to do? Did residents' advisory groups have any real influence in shaping local neighbourhoods? But there were no attempts to assess Unicity's success in creating a new climate for economic growth. Indeed, the first full-scale official review of Unicity made no reference whatever to economic development. The original White Paper had claimed that governmental fragmentation squandered economic capabilities. The review, however, paraphrased that same section of the White paper using these words: "fragmented authority... prevented important decisions from being made and policies from being implemented."[40] The perceived connection between fragmentation and the lack of economic development had, by 1976, apparently been forgotten, if not deliberately ignored.

Ten years later, in 1986, Unicity was once more subject to review by an official committee appointed by the provincial government. Many of the same issues were described and analyzed, but the 1986 review seemed

---

38. Manitoba, *Proposals for Urban Reorganization in the Greater Winnipeg Area* (1970), p. 2.
39. Manitoba, *Proposals* (1970) pp.2-3.
40. Manitoba, Committee of Review, City of Winnipeg Act, *Report and Recommendations* (Winnipeg: Queen's Printer for Manitoba, 1976), p. 9.

broader in its overall scope. There was at least a cursory attempt to assess Unicity's economic impact. The main conclusion was that the Unicity structure, with its many suburban councillors and large tax base, facilitated the building of suburban infrastructure, to the detriment of inner-city investment.[41]

If this assessment is correct – and it certainly matches the conventional wisdom about Winnipeg's post-Unicity development – then it illustrates remarkably well how structural reform can have unintended consequences. The authors of the Unicity scheme assumed that, by equalizing tax levels and services throughout the urbanized Winnipeg area, the relatively well-off suburbs would automatically be forced to subsidize the revitalization of the central city. But they seemed to ignore the fact that the population of the 11 suburban municipalities was greater than that of the old city of Winnipeg[42] and that suburban areas had considerably more growth potential. Assuming representation by population – which was always part of the NDP's plan – suburban dominance within Unicity was inevitable.

The main Unicity consultants for the Manitoba government subsequently defended themselves on this issue by arguing that suburban growth was inevitable under any set of structures and that, if one analyzes Unicity "non-growth" capital expenditures from 1972-1980, "more than 80 per cent of these non-growth expenditures went to the central area, e.g. the former City of Winnipeg."[43] Since there is doubt that low-density suburban growth was very costly, the issues in dispute are the extent to which it was inevitable and who should be paying the infrastructure costs. At a minimum, it would appear that the creation of Unicity facilitated suburban growth, in part by spreading the costs throughout the metropolitan area[44] rather than by concentrating them on the new residents and/or their immediate neighbours within the relatively small suburban municipalities.

Although the 1986 review of Unicity pointed to a lack of coordination between Unicity and the province on strategies for local economic

---

41. Manitoba, City of Winnipeg Act Review Committee, *Final Report 1986*, p. 5. See also, Lloyd Axworthy, "The Best Laid Plans Oft Go Astray: The Case of Winnipeg," in M.O. Dickerson, S. Drabek and J.T. Woods (eds.), *Problems of Change in Urban Government* (Waterloo ON: Wilfrid Laurier University Press, 1980) pp. 105-123.

42. Manitoba, *Urban Reorganization* (1970), p. 12.

43. Brownstone and Plunkett, *Metropolitan Winnipeg*, p. 171.

44. There are no "development charges" or "lot levies" in Winnipeg. For a general explanation and assessment, see Enid Slack and Richard Bird, "Financing Urban Growth through Development Charges," *Canadian Tax Journal* Vol. 39, no. 5 (1991), pp. 1288-1304.

development,[45] there was later some evidence that the situation had improved. In August 1993, *The Globe and Mail Report on Business Magazine* designated Winnipeg as one of Canada's five "best cities for business."[46] Many of the reasons for such a designation were beyond the control of local government: location, cost of living, attributes of the workforce. Premier Gary Filmon "and his tenacious young economic development team" were given credit for being effective salespeople for the city as well as the province. The economic development group in the city was characterized as being "highly organized," while the mayor and the chief commissioner were praised for controlling expenditures and improving the city's credit rating. Despite all this, it was acknowledged that property taxes in Winnipeg "are disproportionately high compared with those of other Canadian cities."[47]

Nowhere in the magazine article is there any claim that Winnipeg might be in an advantageous position because there is only one municipal government covering most of the city-region. There is no evidence that the absence of inter-municipal conflict has made any difference to the pattern of Winnipeg's economic development over the last 20 years. Convincing evidence would be difficult, if not impossible, to collect but, given the kinds of claims made by the original proponents of Unicity, one would think that there should at least be anecdotal reports from the occasional business executive who has found relief in post-1972 Winnipeg from the dreadful burdens of municipal fragmentation. If such reports exist, they have not been reproduced in official government documents or in the academic literature.

The 1986 review of Unicity also addressed problems relating to the wider Winnipeg metropolitan area. In view of past policies favouring amalgamation and consolidation, one surprising recommendation was that the extreme western portion of the city – the Headingley area – be allowed to secede.

> [W]e perceive the area as a predominantly rural area without the status of a rural municipality. It would appear beneficial, therefore, to permit the area to pursue its rural and agricultural future as either a separate municipality or as part of an existing rural municipality. As an important asset in the

---

45. Manitoba, *Final Report* 1986, p.33.
46. Ann Walmsley, "City Lights," (August 1993) p.49. The other four were Moncton, Vancouver, Edmonton, and Montreal.
47. Walmsley, "City Lights," pp.52-3.

Winnipeg region, rural Headingley should be given the opportunity to govern itself within the role that apparently all parties wish it to play.[48]

In 1991 the provincial government conducted a referendum among all residents and property owners in the area. Of 1,390 persons enumerated, 1,163 (83.6 per cent) voted and, of these, 1,008 (86.7 per cent) supported secession and the establishment of a new rural municipality. In 1992 legislation was approved to make this possible.[49] Unicity had become slightly less comprehensive than it was before.

But other factors were also working in this direction. In 1971 the municipalities that were to comprise Unicity accounted for 99.1 per cent of Winnipeg's census metropolitan area (CMA). In 1996 the figure was still high – 92.7 per cent – but it had been significantly reduced. Between 1991 and 1996 the city of Winnipeg's population increased by 0.5 per cent while that of the rest of the CMA outside the city went up by 7.7 per cent. The City of Winnipeg contained 92.7 per cent of the population of Winnipeg's CMA but, between 1991 and 1996, it only accounted for 48.2 per cent of the population growth.[50] In comparison to other Canadian city-regions, these figures for the central municipality are still very impressive, but they do indicate that even with the most comprehensive of structural reforms, much urban-related development takes place outside the central urban municipality.

The 1986 review recognized this by recommending the establishment of a new advisory, consultative, and co-ordinating organization linking all municipalities within the Winnipeg commutershed. The review committee made it clear that it was not recommending "a new layer of regional government as in Ontario." Nor was it recommending "another layer of bureaucracy."[51] Despite these disclaimers, the committee clearly accepted the fact that for some municipal purposes – such as regional planning, environmental assessments, and refuse disposal – the boundaries of Unicity were too limited. The new inter-municipal organization was also seen as having a role in assembling data and co-ordinating research relating to "economic development, industrial location, tourism... and other relevant matters of importance to the region."[52]

---

48. Manitoba, *Final Report* 1986, p.74.
49. Manitoba, Ministry of Urban Affairs, *Annual Report 1991-92* p.40.
50. All population figures on which these calculations are based are found in the relevant federal census publications.
51. Manitoba, *Final Report* 1986, p.77.
52. Manitoba, *Final Report* 1986, p.75.

In 1989 the provincial government established what is now known as the Capital Region Committee. It is co-chaired by the minister of urban affairs and the minister of rural development and it comprises the minister of the environment and the mayors and reeves of the 16 municipalities in the region.[53] In 1998 the Committee established an "independent panel" to conduct a "Capital Region Review." In an interim report in June 1999 the panel stated that

>...the existing legislative, policy and procedural framework in the Region has not been entirely effective. In particular, there is a need to improve regional awareness and thinking; to institute strategic regional planning of those activities which involve region-wide impacts; and to ensure that the costs and benefits of service delivery in the Region are better allocated among the various governments, ratepayers, and residents... [W]e believe that some form of regional agency is required to address these needs. There is a broad spectrum of options available, ranging from a third tier of government to greater collaboration between existing local governments.[54]

What is the lesson from all this? It is that 30 years after Canada's most dramatic and comprehensive municipal amalgamation – in which virtually all the residents of the Winnipeg city-region were included – the area now confronts the same problems as everyone else: most of the growth is occurring outside the municipal boundaries and there is a need for new mechanisms for regional co-operation. No one is recommending further amalgamations. After all, it has only been seven years since Headingley was allowed to leave.

Another lesson is that structural arrangements to encourage citizen participation after amalgamation do not necessarily work. The original 51-member Unicity council now has only 15 members. The community committees and residents' advisory groups [RAGs] have been abolished.[55] Shortly before the decision was made about the community committees, researchers from the Canadian Urban Institute conducted interviews in Winnipeg to determine the effectiveness of the city's apparently innovative mechanisms for citizen participation.

53. Manitoba, Capital Region Review, *Partners for the Future: Working Together to Strengthen Manitoba's Capital Region* (1998), p.3. <http:www.sus-dev.gov.mb.ca/capreg/crpub.html>

54. Manitoba, Capital Region Review, *Interim Panel Report*, 15 July 1999 <http:www.susdev.gov.mb.ca/interimreport/index.html>

55. For an account of city council's actions on 29 October 1997 concerning George B. Cuff's "Organizational Review and Performance Assessment Report" see <http:www.mbnet.mb.ca/city/cuff.htm>

One former councillor interviewed in the course of preparing this report felt there was value in the community committees in that they provided a mechanism for holding councillors publicly accountable for their decisions. All others interviewed supported the more common view that Winnipeg's community committees and RAGs may have made sense in theory, but in practice they have not been effective. To the extent that they do not deliver the community empowerment that they promised in theory, they can be seen as not simply ineffective, but debilitating in their impact on citizen involvement in local affairs.[56]

In 1972 Winnipeg's Unicity was seen as a bold new experiment in municipal government for city-regions. It was territorially comprehensive, administratively centralized, and structured politically to enhance neighbourhood involvement. In 1999, all that is left is the administrative centralization.

EUROPE

During the 1970s, the United Kingdom conducted separate but comprehensive reorganizations involving municipal amalgamations in each of its four constituent nations. We have seen in Canada that only a few provinces became engaged in such reorganizations and those that did – Ontario, Quebec, and Manitoba – acted incrementally, never completely reorganizing municipalities throughout their populated areas. In some European countries the experience was quite different: central governments completely reorganized their sub-national governments all at once. It will be impossible to examine these changes in any detail, in part because local government reorganizations can never be understood in isolation from a good knowledge of the full political and administrative context in which they take place. The European experience is presented here mainly to show that municipal amalgamations in the 1960s and 70s were not restricted to Britain and Canada. The countries in which there were the most significant reductions in the number of municipalities were: Sweden (2,500 in 1950, 279 in 1980); Denmark (1,387 in 1961, 275 in 1974); and West Germany (24,512 in 1959, 8,514 in 1978).[57]

---

56. Eudora Pendergrast and John Farrow, *Community Councils and Neighbour-hood Committees: Lessons for our Communities from around the World* (Toronto: Canadian Urban Institute, 1997), Appendix A-3, p.4.
57. Sharpe, "Local Government Reorganization," p.99.

As in most European countries, Swedish municipalities are pillars of the welfare state. In 1990, their major expenditure items were social services (27.8 per cent of total municipal spending) and education (22.8 per cent). More than half of the funds for each of these services came from local sources, mainly a local income tax that accounted for 63.1 per cent of total local revenue from taxation.[58] Under these circumstances, we can already see that whatever has happened in Sweden, it is unlikely to be of much relevance in Quebec where municipalities have no responsibility for social service or for education and where there is no local income tax. Nevertheless, the amalgamated municipalities have been seen as more self-sufficient, more effective in planning, and better able to deliver services equitably over large areas than their fragmented predecessors.[59] But, even after such a dramatic program of municipal amalgamations, there remain 20 separate municipalities within the area of Greater Stockholm.[60]

Two recent studies have been conducted about the effects of the amalgamations on municipal costs. The first, published in 1992, found that the first wave of amalgamations, which increased the average population of Swedish municipalities from 2,800 to 6,800 inhabitants, did indeed lead to reduced costs. The same study found that the second wave resulted in increased spending.[61] Another study published in 1997 looked at spending patterns in the amalgamated municipalities and found a significant positive association between population and per capita spending. The author commented:

> The unwieldy nature of large bureaucracies seems to outweigh economies of scale. We should keep in mind, however, that the data set does not shed any light on the relationship between spending and population size for municipalities smaller than the smallest municipality in the sample...The smallest municipality in the sample, Vaxholm, is, with 7,000 inhabitants, very close in size to the average municipality after the first mergers.[62]

---

58. David E. Andersson, "Regions and the Collectivity: Swedish Local Government and the Case of Stockholm" in A.E. Andersson, B. Harsman, and J.M. Quigley, eds., *Governments for the Future - Unification, Fragmentation and Regionalism* (Elsevier Science, 1997), p.267.
59. Alan Norton, *International Handbook of Local and Regional Government: A Comparative Analysis of Advanced Democracies* (Aldershot, Hants.: Edward Elgar, 1994), p.299.
60. Norton, *International Handbook*, p.319.
61. M.A. Nelson, "Municipal Amalgamation and the Growth of the Local Public Sector in Sweden," *Journal of Regional Science*, 32 (1992).
62. Andersson, "Regions and the Collectivity," p.273.

Most of what has been stated above about Sweden also applies to Denmark, except that there appears to have been no published Danish studies about the relationship between municipal size and costs. Even after all the amalgamations implemented in 1970, the average population for a Danish municipality in the mid 1990s was only 18,000.[63] The equivalent figure for *lower-tier* local authorities in England was 126,000 (46,000,000 divided by 365). Such a difference demonstrates just one of the many pitfalls of comparative local government. Consolidated Denmark is still more than 10 times more fragmented than consolidated England.

Germany, like Canada and the United States, is a federation in which the "länder", (equivalents of provinces and states) have jurisdiction over local government. This means there have been different approaches to municipal amalgamation in different parts of the country. Once again, however, North Americans must be careful in applying their own conceptions about the nature of municipal government to a country in Europe. Consider this account of amalgamation issues in Germany:

> Länder set up their own commissions to work out the principles of reorganisation. Norms were set up with functional needs in mind. In North Rhine-Westphalia, the needs that determined the set minimum of 8,000 included a primary school with gymnasium and swimming pool for learners, an old people's home and a pharmacy. At a minimum size of 30,000 a secondary school, a school for the handicapped, an abattoir and a cultural centre were considered possible.[64]

Even in North America's rural areas, students and practitioners need not concern themselves with drawing local government boundaries based on the service areas of abattoirs.

Just as it is wrong to assume that amalgamation frenzy swept all Canadian provinces in the 1960s and 1970s, it is also wrong to assume that it swept all European countries. In 1950, Italy had 7,810 municipalities, in 1972 there were 8,056; Greece had 5,993 in 1962 and 6,037 in 1979; France had 37,708 in 1968 and 36,423 in 1980.[65] The alternatives to amalgamation were similar in various jurisdictions. Italy, Greece, and France have all established new forms of regional institutions without disturbing traditional municipal boundaries. In all these cases municipalities

---

63. Kurt Klaudi Klausen, "Danish Local Government: Integrating into the EU?" in M.J.F. Goldsmith and K.K. Klausen, eds., *European Integration and Local Government* (Cheltenham: Edward Elgar, 1997), p.17.

64. Norton, *International Handbook*, p.252.

65. Sharpe, "Local Government Reorganisation," p.99.

tend to carry on doing what they have traditionally done; they are not large enough to take on new functions on their own, and so these tend to go by default to the regional institutions. The old municipalities tend to perform important representative and political functions and they look after issues that are genuinely local; they tend not to be on the cutting edge of new government initiatives.

TABLE 2: NUMBER OF MUNICIPALITIES IN EUROPEAN COUNTRIES MOST AND LEAST AFFECTED BY MUNICIPAL AMALGAMATIONS

COUNTRIES MOST AFFECTED

	1950S &1960S	1970S	LATE 1980S
SWEDEN	2,500 (1950)	279 (1980)	284
DENMARK	1,387 (1961)	275 (1974)	273
WEST GERMANY	24,512 (1959)	8,514 (1978)	8,846

COUNTRIES LEAST AFFECTED

	1950S &1960S	1970S	LATE 1980S
ITALY	7,810 (1950)	8,506 (1972)	8,074
GREECE	5,993 (1962)	6,037 (1979)	6,022
FRANCE	37,708 (1968)	36,423 (1980)	36,757

SOURCES: Figures from the first two columns are from Sharpe, "Local Government Reorganisation," p.99; for the last column, from Norton, *International Handbook*, p.40.

CONCLUSION

Advocates of municipal amalgamation in the 1960s and 1970s believed that their preferred approach to government organization would make an important difference in the quality of urban services and of our urban environment. They were not especially concerned about financial matters, but sometimes they often claimed that "in the long term" savings would be apparent. In 1999, we can safely say that in relation to these claims at least, "the long run" has arrived. What are the benefits that amalgamations have brought? How are areas that have been amalgamated better off than those that have not? How has amalgamation helped Winnipeg? Is it better to live in Laval than in Greenfield Park? If so, is it because Laval is so much bigger? These are the kinds of questions that need to be asked as we experience a renewed interest in municipal amalgamations. Unfortunately, they rarely are.

The municipal amalgamations of the 1960s and 1970s were the result of an optimistic belief that larger local governments could lead to new and better ways of doing things. The evidence suggested otherwise. There was a feeling by the mid-1970s that solving local problems by creating bigger governments simply did not work. The old assumptions seemed to be breaking down. No one really believed them anymore. Both a cause and effect of this loss of faith in bigness was the emergence in the United States of a new way of thinking about urban governance.

CHAPTER 3

THE DECLINE OF THE CONSOLIDATIONIST MOVEMENT IN THE UNITED STATES, THE EMERGENCE OF "PUBLIC CHOICE," AND THE "NEW REGIONALISM"

F or most of the second half of the twentieth century American cities have been objects of scorn rather than of emulation. In their governance they have been remarkably fragmented. Attempts at municipal consolidation have generally failed, and some have seen such failures as being both the cause and effect of their often disastrous conditions. As with so much of American life and culture, the state of their cities has generated a rich academic and popular literature, some of it directly concerned with the issue of municipal consolidation. This chapter reviews this literature with the aim of clarifying what is relevant to Canadian debates and what is not. In current political debate in Canada about municipal structures, there are frequent references to the American experience, but many are quite misleading or outrightly false.

This chapter contains three sections arranged roughly in chronological order, each following a different current in the American literature. That is not to say, however, that there is no overlap or threads of common concern. On the contrary, one theme leads to another in an almost dialectical process: hypothesis, contradiction, synthesis. The first theme is a continuation of what we examined in Chapter 1 – efforts by consolidationists to redraw the municipal maps of American city-regions. The differences in the 1950s and 1960s were that there were many more attempts and many more failures, most of them carefully documented and analysed by the growing number of political scientists and urban experts who were filling social science faculties in American universities. The second section in the chapter shows how their work was eventually eclipsed by economists intent on showing that consolidationist fervour was completely misplaced. According to this line of thought – the "public choice" school – city-regions were better off with many municipal governments than with few. In fact, municipalities, according to this approach, should be seen more as competing organizers of different bundles of taxes and public services rather than as governments in the traditional sense. Just as consumers benefit from competition among retail grocery stores, property owners should benefit from similar competion among municipalities. Finally, in the 1990s, there has been a renewed interest in looking at the overall health of entire city-regions. Perhaps because of the influence of "public choice," few of the "new regionalists" have been much interested in large-scale structural consolidation.

MUNICIPAL CONSOLIDATION IN THE U.S. SINCE 1945

Strictly speaking, this should be a very short section: there have been no municipal consolidations in the United States since 1910 analogous to those in Philadelphia and New York (and Winnipeg), in which the state (or provincial) legislature used its authority to merge all the municipalities in a city-region into one. In fact, the total number of incorporated municipalities (excluding counties and townships) in the United States increased from 16,807 in 1952 to 19,372 in 1997.[1] Although it is true that the territories of many central cities and suburban municipalities have grown in this period, especially in the southern and western parts of the country, such growth has resulted from a few cases of municipalities themselves deciding to merge with each other and from many more in which unincorporated areas were annexed by adjoining municipalities. In most cases, no annexations have taken place without the approval, by referendum, of the affected residents.

Nor have many upper-tier metropolitan governments been created. In Miami in 1957, the functional responsibility of Dade county was extended, making it look similar in some respects to the Municipality of Metropolitan Toronto. But even in Dade county, police patrol remained a lower-tier municipal function.[2] Since 1967 there has been a Twin Cities Metropolitan Council covering seven cities and 130 municipalities around Minneapolis-St. Paul, but its functions have been limited to a form of region-wide

---

1. United States, Department of Commerce, U.S. Census Bureau, *1997 Census of Governments, Vol.1, Government Organization* (August 1999), p.5. These figures exclude counties and townships, the latter being a form of sub-county institution existing in many northern states.
2. John J. Harrigan, *Political Change in the Metropolis*, 5th ed. (New York: Harper-Collins, 1993), pp.354-6.

strategic planning. All of its 17 members are appointed by the state governor.[3] Since 1978, Portland, Oregon, has had a 12-member, directly-elected Metropolitan Service District responsible for regional land-use planning, sewage treatment, solid-waste disposal, flood control and the zoo.[4] This completes the list of institutionalized upper-tier metropolitan governments in the United States. In none of these cases has the establishment of the upper tier been accompanied by any lower-tier amalgamations.

Most of the municipal restructuring battles since 1945 in the United States have related to proposals to merge a central city to the "unincorporated" areas of the county that surrounds it. Americans call such a merger "city-county consolidation" even when incorporated suburban municipalities are not included, which they almost never are. Since 1945 there have only been three city-county consolidations involving more than 250,000 people: Nashville and Davidson county in 1962; Jacksonville and Duval county in 1967; and Indianapolis and Marion county in 1969. Four incorporated suburban municipalities continue to exist within Jacksonville and six within Nashville. In both Jacksonville and Nashville, the mergers were approved in referendums, in large measure because the county was incapable of providing proper services.[5] By the standards of any other country, including Canada, these were not really consolidations at all; they were large-scale annexations that just happened to include all of a county, rather than just part of one.

This leaves one significant post-war American case: Indianapolis. The "Unigov" system in Indianapolis was created by the Indiana state legislature in 1969 without any approval by local referendums. Once again, by the standards of any other country, this is a most peculiar form of "unified" government. The Unigov system merged the executive branches of the city of Indianapolis and of Marion county, but each remains as a separate legal entity because of provisions in the Indiana state constitution. Seventeen small incorporated towns, all with populations under 5,000, were "included" in the Unigov system but, "[t]hese communities may maintain governments,

3. Judith J. Martin, "Renegotiating Metropolitan Consciousness: The Twin Cities Faces its Future," in Donald N. Rothblatt and Andrew Sancton, eds. *Metropolitan Governance Revisited: Canadian-American Intergovernmental Perspectives* (Berkeley: Institute of Governmental Studies Press at the University of California, 1998), p.238. See also, Claire Poitras et Richard Lanthier sous la direction de Jean-Pierre Collin et Jacques Léveillée, "La fiscalité d'agglomération au Canada et États-Unis: Analyse de cinq agglomérations urbaines," remis à la Conférence des maires de la banlieue de Montréal, 9 octobre 1998, pp.43-55.
4. Harrigan, *Political Change*, p.350-1.
5. Harrigan, *Political Change*, p.350-1.

levy property taxes, and provide local services in addition to those provided by the city and county."[6]

Nine townships within Marion county also continue to exist. The townships are governed by elected trustees whose main functions relate to fire protection, "poor relief," and tax assessment. Four incorporated municipalities with populations of more than 5,000 were quite unaffected by the introduction of the new system, relying on Unigov only for services traditionally provided by counties. Finally, existing special-purpose bodies, including 11 different school boards, were also unaffected. In 1995, two academic observers of the Unigov system wrote:

> Although the 'Unigov' nickname stands for 'unified government,' Marion County retains 50 separate local governments (down from 60 in 1967) and the number of separate taxing units in the county has grown since 1970 to approximately 100. In some respects, the Unigov structure is even more complicated than that which it replaced.[7]

Indianapolis-Marion County does not even have a consolidated police department:

> ... the Indianapolis Police Department... serves the Police Special Service District, an area somewhat larger than the 'old city' but not as extensive as the Consolidated City. Outside the Police Special Services District, Marion County residents receive police protection from the Marion County Sheriff's Department or from the municipal force of an excluded city.[8]

Important as it is to know about post-war American experience with the governance of city-regions, the harsh fact is that there have been no American consolidations of the type experienced in Canada, Britain, and Europe. American experience with municipal consolidation is relevant only in the sense that it shows us what happens when municipal consolidations do not take place.

Most American city-regions contain dozens of municipalities and few see this as any kind of problem. Perhaps the best way to understand the relevance of the American situation for Montreal is to compare the Montreal

---

6. William Blomquist and Roger B. Parks, "Unigov: Local Government in Indianapolis and Marion County, Indiana," in L.J. Sharpe, ed. *The Government of World Cities: The Future of the Metro Model* (Chichester, England: John Wiley and Sons, 1995), p.80.

7. Blomquist and Parks, "Unigov," p.81.

8. Blomquist and Parks, "Unigov," pp.80-1.

city-region with American ones of similar size. Table 3 (below) looks at the municipal make-up of the 18 American city-regions that are closest in population to Montreal's, nine larger and nine smaller.

TABLE 3: MUNICIPAL CHARACTERISTICS OF MONTREAL AND AMERICAN CITY-REGIONS OF SIMILAR SIZE

CITY-REGION	POPULATION (000S)	POPULATION IN CENTRAL CITY (%)	NUMBER OF COUNTIES	NUMBER OF MUNICIPALITIES*
SAN FRANCISCO	6,701	10.9	9	90
PHILADELPHIA	5,972	26.0	13	230
BOSTON	5,828	9.5	12	282
DETROIT	5,439	18.6	10	151
DALLAS	4,683	21.8	12	207
HOUSTON	4,320	39.1	8	115
ATLANTA	3,627	10.9	20	102
MIAMI	3,515	10.4	2	55
SEATTLE	3,368	15.4	6	88
MONTREAL	3,327	30.5	**17	111
CLEVELAND	2,908	17.3	8	146
PHOENIX	2,840	35.6	2	32
MINNEAPOLIS	2,792	13.0	13	192
SAN DIEGO	2,723	42.2	1	18
ST. LOUIS	2,558	15.0	11	228
PITTSBURGH	2,361	15.5	6	238
DENVER	2,318	20.9	6	67
TAMPA	2,227	12.8	4	35
PORTLAND	2,113	21.1	8	79

*excludes townships, except in the Boston area where townships perform the same functions as multi-purpose municipal governments, including towns.

**The MUC is treated as a single county.

SOURCES: American data constructed from various links on the U.S.Census Bureau website: <http:www.census.gov>. Montreal data from the 1996 Canadian census as reported in Quebec, *Pacte 2000: Rapport de la Commission nationale sur les finances et la fiscalité locales* (1999), p.182. The assistance of Andrew Ross of the city of Westmount in creating this table is greatly appreciated.

The Montreal city-region looks quite typical, except that the city of Montreal has a relatively high proportion of the city-region's population. It is important to note also that none of the American city-regions has an upper-tier metropolitan government that has anything approaching the degree of functional and financial strength possessed by the Montreal Urban Community. For example, policing in the United States is never an upper-tier function.

PUBLIC CHOICE

This is not the place to attempt a full description and analysis of public-choice as it relates to municipal government.[9] The key point is that public choice – which emerged from economics departments in American universities in the 1960s and 1970s – offers a quite different paradigm for city-region governance from that of the consolidationists. Public-choice analysts insist that there is no functionally optimal size for municipal governments because different municipal activities have quite different optimal areas. For example, police patrol is optimally organized for relatively small areas because there are few economies of scale; homicide squads and police-training facilities require larger territories because there are significant economies of scale. In any event, municipalities work best when they arrange for service provision, not when they always insist on producing all municipal services themselves.

Within the public-choice paradigm, we should no more worry about too many municipalities than we should worry about too many firms involved in the retailing of groceries. Just as different grocery stores provide different levels of selection, quality, and price, so too do municipalities. Having one municipality responsible for providing all the municipal services in a city-region makes as much sense as having one monopoly grocery firm. The firm might promise to open many stores in many different locations, but it would still be a monopoly.

---

9. The most useful starting points are: Robert L. Bish and Vincent Ostrom, *Understanding Urban Government: Metropolitan Reform Reconsidered* (Washington DC: American Enterprise Institute for Public Policy Research, 1973); Vincent Ostrom, Robert Bish, and Elinor Ostrom, *Local Government in the United States* (San Francisco: Institute for Contemporary Studies Press, 1988) and Ronald J. Oakerson, *Governing Local Public Economies: Creating the Civic Metropolis* (San Francisco: Institute for Contemporary Studies Press, 1999).

Questions about the public-choice position are always quick to emerge. Are residents of a particular municipality really likely to move because they are dissatisfied with services and taxes? Do they even know much about relative service levels and taxes in different places? What about large-scale regional planning? How can this be possible if there is no authoritative metropolitan government? What about fiscal equity? Is public choice not just a mechanism that enables the rich to escape paying for services to the poor?

Public-choice defenders have, of course, worked out their answers, some more satisfactory than others. Competition, they say, is always an important motivator for organizations, even if only very few people might move as a result of their own personal assessments of different municipal levels of services and taxes. Large-scale regional planning has not had much real effect in altering how city-regions develop. In any event, if it is to be coercive, it is best done at the state or provincial level; if it is to be co-operative, there is no need to build elaborate new structures. Redistributing wealth is a function best performed by higher levels of government, not by local governments. Even big local governments committed to redistribution will – like New York City in the 1970s – ultimately discover that extensive redistribution at the local level cannot be sustained.

We need not decide whether public choice is right or wrong. The point is that it gives us good reason to at least question the consolidationist paradigm. The public-choice perspective shows us that it is no longer obvious that the existence of many municipalities within the same city-region causes wasteful overlap and duplication. To be intellectually convincing, consolidationists must now specify exactly what it is that they expect a consolidation to accomplish, and why this objective cannot better be achieved by following some other course of action. With the possible exception of David Rusk (discussed in the next section), consolidationists have not responded.

In addition to developing an alternative theoretical paradigm, public-choice scholars have done considerable research relating to how local governments in multi-municipal city-regions actually get things done. The most comprehensive of these studies were carried out in St. Louis and Pittsburgh in the late 1980s and early 1990s for the U.S. federal government's Advisory Council on Intergovernmental Relations (ACIR). Each of these studies will be treated in turn.

The St. Louis study was concerned only with the city of St. Louis and St. Louis county that surrounds it. It virtually ignores 10 other counties that are part of the city-region for census purposes. In 1996, the total population of the St. Louis metropolitan statistical area was 2,558,000. The city's population was 368,000 and the county's 1,003,000: almost half the city-region's population was outside the area being studied. St. Louis city and county are to the St. Louis city-region much as the Montreal Urban Community (MUC) is to the Montreal city-region. The main differences are that the city of Montreal is far more populous and dominant that the city of St. Louis and that St. Louis county contained 90 incorporated municipalities while suburban areas of the MUC contained only 28.[10]

In 1954, city and county residents voted by a margin of 3 to 1 to establish a joint Metropolitan St. Louis Sewer District. Subsequent proposals for other forms of metropolitan special-purpose bodies were defeated, although there is now a Metropolitan Zoological Park and Museum District.[11] In short, there is very little in the way of formal institutional arrangements holding the area together.

The most detailed analysis in the ACIR study was done for police and fire services. In 1988, 63 of the 90 county municipalities had their own police departments. The rest contracted from another municipality or from the county. An analysis of police costs within county municipalities concluded that:

> Some slight economies of scale are enjoyed by the larger police departments... In the per capita equations, the coefficients indicate that, after adjustment for other factors affecting police expenditures, a 1,000 resident increase... is predicted to yield a decrease of somewhat less than one per cent [50-70 cents a year per capita] for an average department.
>
> The effect of size is relatively weak, however... [T]he presence of business activity has the greatest effect on police expenditures.[12]

All county departments used the county's crime laboratory and all departments in both the city and the county relied on the Greater St. Louis Police Academy for training.[13] Various departments contracted with each other for specialized services. All police departments in the metropolitan area (including some in southern Illinois) participated in the Major Case Squad, which operates under the auspices of the Board of Governors of

---

10. Data for St. Louis is from the website of the U.S. census bureau.
11. United States, Advisory Council on Intergovernmental Relations (ACIR), *Metropolitan Organization: The St. Louis Case*, Report M-181(1988), pp. 27 and 36.
12. ACIR, *St. Louis*, p.59.
13. ACIR, *St. Louis*, p.60.

the Law Enforcement Officials of the Greater St. Louis Area. It is concerned primarily with the investigation of homicides.[14]

Twenty municipalities in the city and county had their own fire departments; five contracted with other municipalities; and three contracted from fire service districts. The remaining 62 municipalities were participating members of 24 fire districts, but one fire district contracts for services from a neighbouring municipality.[15] Economies of scale were apparent for fire services up to a population level of 50,000, but there were no economies of scale according to the total value of property protected.[16] Numerous examples of co-operation were discovered, including mutual aid agreements, common recruiting standards and programs, joint training exercises, central inventory listing for emergencies, and, for many departments, joint arrangements for dispatch. Operationally, the system seemed to work well. Most conflicts among fire departments resulted from annexations of unincorporated county areas by nearby municipalities. This sometimes had the effect of reducing the resources of fire districts and provoked them temporarily to suspend mutual aid agreements to the affected areas.[17]

Claims are often made that municipal fragmentation in a metropolitan area hinders economic development. The ACIR study presented data to show that as many new jobs were created in St. Louis in the preceding years as in other American metropolitan areas of similar size and with similar economic bases. The data suggested that the number of municipal governments in an area was unconnected to the number of new jobs created. However, the study's authors acknowledged that because of the complete institutional separation between the county and the city, downtown St. Louis might have lost out on the kind of suburban assistance and partnerships that have been available in other cities where county jurisdiction includes the central city.[18] In general, however, the overall assessment of the St. Louis system by the ACIR study was very positive.

Like the St. Louis study, the ACIR study of Pittsburgh was only concerned with the central city and county. It ignored five surrounding counties that made up the Pittsburgh metropolitan statistical area, whose population in 1996 was 2,361,000. The city's population was 367,000 and the rest of Allegheny county's was 929,000. Within Allegheny county there

---

14. ACIR, *St. Louis*, p.63.
15. ACIR, *St. Louis*, p.69.
16. ACIR, *St. Louis*, p.72.
17. ACIR, *St. Louis*, p.74.
18. ACIR, *St. Louis*, p.121.

were 86 incorporated municipalities and 42 townships, each with its own elected council.

The findings of the ACIR study for Pittsburgh were similar to those for St. Louis. The Allegheny County Sanitary Authority provided sewage collection and treatment for Pittsburgh and many county municipalities. The Municipal Authority of the Borough of West View provided water services to Allegheny and adjacent counties.[19] There were more than 100 separate police departments, yet police costs in Allegheny county were below the average for other American urban areas of similar size.[20] More than 250 separate organizations – most of them volunteer – provided fire protection.[21] The study concluded in these words:

> The most prominent organizational features of Allegheny County are not functional fragmentation, inefficiency, and inequity, but public entrepreneurship, community-based organization and voluntarism, and intergovernmental problem-solving.[22]

Thirty years ago, the obvious response to such an account of local government in Pittsburgh would have been that *something* must be wrong because the whole area was in severe economic decline, a rustbelt disaster if there ever was one. As the 20th century ends, however, Pittsburgh is experiencing a remarkable renaissance. The reasons for its recovery relate only indirectly to the structural arrangements of municipal government. But the fact that it could recover without municipal consolidation is an important point to consider. We turn now to some of the factors that are more directly related to its recovery and to similar recoveries in other American cities.

NEW REGIONALIST APPROACHES IN THE U.S.

Just when it seemed that the municipal consolidationist movement was dead in the United States, it emerged again in another form. The core political values of most American consolidationists involved fairness, equity, and openness. They believed that government was generally a force for

---

19. ACIR, *Metropolitan Organization: The Allegheny County Case*, Report M-181 (1992), p.16.
20. ACIR, *Allegheny*, p.41.
21. ACIR, *Allegheny*, p.47.
22. ACIR, *Allegheny*, p.88.

good and that, in some respects at least, it was more effective than the marketplace. These same values are at the heart of a growing trend in the United States to look at cities in their full regional context. With one exception, most of the advocates of new regional approaches have been more concerned with results than with structures, more interested in partnerships than in mergers. None of them accepts all the assumptions and values of public choice, but they avoid the trap of arguing that bigger local governments are naturally more efficient.

This discussion of new regionalist thinking in the U.S. will begin with David Rusk, the one author in this group who is interested in municipal boundaries. Rusk was mayor of Albuquerque, New Mexico, from 1977 to 1981. He later held senior positions under President Clinton in the federal Department of Housing and Urban Development. Like most of the new regionalists, Rusk is what Americans would consider a "liberal;" he is certainly no advocate of further cuts to government expenditures for renewing American cities. Perhaps this explains why he is so rarely cited in Canadian debates about municipal amalgamation, debates that have recently been prompted more by an apparent desire to reduce the size of government than to expand it. Another reason may be that Rusk's main priority seems to be to reduce disparities between well-off white suburbanites and inner-city visible minorities, a priority that seems not to be so pressing in Canada.

In any event, Rusk's book, *Cities without Suburbs*, first published in 1993 and reissued in a second edition in 1995, has been a significant factor in placing the issue of municipal boundaries back on the American liberal agenda, if not the national agenda. Rusk's main argument is that cities that have been able to expand their boundaries significantly since 1950 ("elastic" cities) are less racially segregated than those that have not. He also presents data showing that the economies of city-regions whose central cities are elastic are better off than those with inelastic central cities. The problem here, as Rusk acknowledges himself, is that sunbelt areas (including Alburquerque) generally have state laws that make annexation of unincorporated areas relatively easy, while in older (and colder) parts of the country there is less unincorporated territory, and annexation is more procedurally difficult anyway. Rusk thinks the organization of municipalities makes a difference, but he acknowledges that other factors are at work as well.[23]

---

23. David Rusk, *Cities without Suburbs*, 2nd ed. (Washington DC: Woodrow Wilson Centre Press, 1995), pp.66-72.

Before anyone begins applying Rusk's analysis to Canadian cities in general, or Montreal in particular, four important points have to be taken into account. The first is that most Canadian central cities, including Montreal, have increased their territory significantly since 1950. Montreal has annexed the municipalities of Rivière-des-Prairies (1963), Saraguay (1964), Saint-Michel (1968), and Pointe-aux-Trembles (1982). Since it is not clear how Rusk constructed his elasticity index, we cannot calculate Montreal's rating. We do know, however, that it is not zero, the category for New York, Boston, St. Louis, Detroit, Washington DC, Pittsburgh, Cleveland, Baltimore, Minneapolis, Chicago, San Francisco, Philadelphia, Buffalo, and Cincinnati.[24]

The second point is that because the MUC does have authority with respect to regional land-use planning and because policing, public transit, sewage treatment, and economic development are MUC functions, the city of Montreal and its island suburbs are already – even by Rusk's standards – remarkably integrated, both functionally and fiscally. As we have already seen, there is no metropolitan, upper-tier government in the U.S. that is as functionally powerful as the MUC. If the MUC were in the United States, there is little doubt that Rusk would have pointed to it as an example of how metropolitan institutions can be used to help ease centre-city financial burdens. However, he would likely want to extend its fiscal equalization and planning functions beyond its current territorial boundaries.

The third important point is that, if Rusk were making policy in Canada, he would have to take account of the fact that our provinces are much more interventionist in local affairs than American states are. There are no American equivalents of our ministries of municipal affairs, whose mission it is develop policy as to how municipalities are to be structured, financed, and controlled. There are also few, if any, state laws that are as strong as those in Quebec and British Columbia relating to the protection of agricultural land. Although Rusk advocates more state involvement in urban affairs, it is likely that state involvement at levels similar to most Canadian provinces (including Quebec) would cause him to be much less committed to structural change.

Finally, with respect to Rusk, we must realize that among those committed to new regional approaches in the U.S., he is very much in the minority when it comes to advocating dramatic structural change. In advocacy books that have been at least as influential as Rusk's, Neal R.

24.Rusk, *Cities without Suburbs*, pp.138-9.

Peirce,[25] William R. Dodge,[26] and Myron Orfield,[27] all call for new approaches to bringing cities and suburbs together, without ever mentioning the need to change municipal boundaries. They all advocate various combinations of revenue sharing, regional strategic planning, and public-private partnerships, but none says that this requires the creation of larger municipalities.

Among academics, one of the most committed scholars of the political process in American city-regions is H.V. Savitch of the University of Louisville. In 1996 he co-edited a volume of essays entitled *Regional Politics*. It contained no reference to recent amalgamation battles, because there have been none to describe. There are many accounts of failures and difficulties that have developed in various places because governments at all levels have not been able to get along with each other. Perhaps the most remarkable essay in the book is the one about Pittsburgh. The author, Louise Jezierski, begins by stating:

> Fifty years of effort by one of the country's most formidable public-private partnerships has created a new Pittsburgh... Pittsburgh was once a mighty manufacturing region of machinery and primary metals. It is now a "postindustrial" economy centered on "specialized advanced services" catering to the needs of a headquarters city and expanding into high technology sectors of software, engineering, medicine, and education... Pittsburgh is more [municipally] fragmented than any other metropolitan area.[28]

The essay is a remarkable description of a sequence of events that includes industrial growth, the defeat of city-county consolidation by voters in 1929, and the role of private business interests (especially the Mellon family) in working with local politicians to bring about crucial new investment. The author specifically attacks the "public choice" analysis of Pittsburgh for ignoring the high-level political alliances that transcended inter-municipal arrangements for the delivery of routine services. Her point is that Pittsburgh's renaissance did not just emerge from the magic of the

---

25. Neal R, Peirce, *Citistates: How Urban America Can Prosper in a Competitive World* (Washington DC: Seven Locks Press, 1993).

26. William R, Dodge, *Regional Excellence: Governing Together to Compete Globally and Flourish Locally* (Washington DC: National League of Cities, 1996).

27. Myron Orfield, *Metropolitics: A Regional Agenda for Community and Stability*, rev. ed. (Washington DC: Brookings Institution Press, 1997).

28. "Pittsburgh: Partnerships in a Regional City" in H.V. Savitch and Ronald K. Vogel, eds, *Regional Politics: America in a Post-City Age*, Urban Affairs Annual Reviews 45, Thousand Oaks CA: SAGE, 1996), p.159.

marketplace: "The process has been one of conflict, experimentation, sacrifice and loss, a furious level of organization building, and mobilization of consent."[29]

CONCLUSION

There are three conclusions to be drawn from this chapter. First, since 1898 there have been no comprehensive municipal amalgamations in the United States as we understand the concept in Canada. Second, public-choice analysis shows us that the efficient delivery of municipal services does not require large municipalities. Third, a reading of the new regionalist literature in the United States should teach us that the problem with Canadian city-regions is not that they are deficient in formal municipal structures or that they lack provincial involvement. Most Canadian city-regions – including Montreal – already possess many of the governmental institutions that American "new regionalists" advocate. What is missing in Canada is an understanding throughout our society that the economic and social health of our cities is a responsibility of all those with the resources to bring about change. Improving the quality of life in our city-regions is not just a responsibility of those who sit on municipal councils or in provincial legislatures. It is equally a responsibility of the major economic interests based in our various urban areas. Incorporating such interests into our urban policy-making processes without surrendering the final decision-making authority of elected politicians is an extremely messy and delicate undertaking. But it is a process that will ultimately be far more productive than our continuous battles about ideal structures and boundaries for municipal government.

29.Jezierski, "Pittsburgh," p.179.

CHAPTER 4

AMALGAMATIONS IN THE 1990s

During the 1980s in the western industrialized world – including Canada – the subject of municipal amalgamations was not prominent on the political agenda. But in the 1990s, some central governments saw municipal amalgamations as a means to reduce the size of government and to promote economic development. Municipal consolidation was back on the agenda, but this time we heard relatively little about how amalgamations could equalize services and taxes and facilitate regional planning and infrastructure development. Priorities were different in the 1990s and the case for consolidation was adjusted accordingly.

The story begins in the late 1980s in New Zealand, the country that has epitomized government downsizing, deregulation, and reorganization. Subsequent sections in this chapter deal with Australia, Britain, Nova Scotia (especially Halifax), and Ontario (but excluding Toronto, the subject of the next chapter).

Unlike the situation in the 1960s and 1970s, the amalgamations of the 1990s seem isolated to only a few jurisdictions. There is no trend pervading all advanced liberal democracies or, for that matter, even all Canadian provinces. Proposals for rural amalgamations have been specifically rejected in Manitoba and Saskatchewan.[1] A task force charged with examining municipal organization in the Edmonton area has eliminated a "megacity" solution.[2] British Columbia carries on as before – no amalgamations without local agreement. As we review the apparent resurgence of interest in amalgamations in the 1990s, we must constantly keep in mind that this is not a phenomenon that can be found everywhere.

---

1. Joseph Garcea, "Saskatchewan's Aborted Municipal Service Districts Act (Bill33): Pegasus or Trojan Horse," paper presented to the annual meeting of the Canadian Political Science association, St. John's, Newfoundland, June 1997.
2. Alberta Capital Region Review <http://www.acrgr.org/default.cfm>

Perhaps the most intriguing questions relate to why amalgamations have been on the agenda in some places but not others.

NEW ZEALAND

The restructuring of local government in New Zealand in 1989 accompanied a complete overhaul of the national government, one so extensive that it has attracted a great deal of attention for a country with a population of only 3.6 million. One way of looking at the municipal restructuring is to emphasize that the 249 municipalities that existed in 1975 were consolidated into 74 by 1995.[3] But this is too simplistic. Prior to 1989, New Zealand had no intermediate level of government between the national and the local governments. As a result of the 1989 reforms, New Zealand now has 12 directly elected regional councils (not included in the total of 74 municipalities referred to above) whose functions "can be summarised as the regulation of the natural environment with particular emphasis on resource management."[4] Four of the regional councils contain only one municipality and are therefore effectively unitary authorities (just as the city of Laval is itself considered a *municipalité régionale de comté* in Quebec).

There is no question but that the New Zealand reforms were very much concerned with decentralization. Nevertheless, police, fire protection, and public education remain as national government functions, perhaps because by Canadian standards, population levels are low. The largest regional council, Auckland, has a population of 982,000 while the smallest has only 33,000. Within the Auckland region, the population of the central city is only 321,000, even after all the restructuring. There are six other incorporated municipalities. Within the territories of the seven municipalities are 29 elected "community boards," whose functions are purely advisory.[5]

Changes in New Zealand were so extensive in the late 1980s and early 1990s that it would be exceptionally difficult to isolate the effects of the municipal reorganization. Certainly not everybody was happy. Until closed off by new legislation in 1992, secessionist movements to establish new regions and new municipalities were rampant. In this regard, in 1994 the country's "...Controller and Auditor-General commented that valid

3. Graham Bush, *Local Government and Politics in New Zealand*, 2nd ed. (Auckland: Auckland University Press, 1995), pp. 41 and 112.
4. Bush, *New Zealand*, pp.117-8.
5. Bush, *New Zealand*, pp.114-21.

comparisons between pre and post 1989 local bodies as regards costs of services were impossible and that predictions about the performance of proposed breakaway authorities could only be conjecture."[6]

AUSTRALIA

As in New Zealand, local governments in Australia do not do very much. As Peter Self has pointed out, "In Canada and Germany local governments raise almost three times as much revenue as Australian local governments."[7] There is no local spending or control for police or public education. In fact, the main institutions of urban government in Australia are the state governments and their associated public authorities.[8]

Despite their relative lack of functional strength, Australian municipalities have been constantly subjected to pressure from state governments to amalgamate with each other. A recent essay on the subject by Anne Vince begins with these words:

> Amalgamation is a thread which runs through Australian local government history. From 1910 to 1991 the number of federally registered local government authorities, or councils, in Australia decreased from 1,067 to 826... In New South Wales there are now 177 councils compared with 309 in 1937. This diminution in the number of local councils in Australia is almost exclusively attributable to a program of amalgamations in every state.[9]

A recent, apparently successful, campaign for municipal consolidation has taken place since 1992 in Tasmania. The number of municipalities has been reduced from 46 to 29.[10] The total population of Tasmania in 1992 was 470,000.

---

6. Bush, *New Zealand*, pp.105.
7. "The Future of Australian Local Government" in Brian Dollery and Neil Marshall, eds., *Australian Local Government: Reform and Renewal* (Melbourne: Macmillan Education Australia, 1997), p.298.
8. Andrew Parkin, *Governing the Cities: The Australian Experience in Perspective* (South Melbourne, Macmillan of Australia, 1982), p.59.
9. Anne Vince, "Amalgamations" in Dollery and Marshall, eds., *Australian Local Government*, p.151.
10. Vince, "Amalgamations," p.161.

In the state of Victoria, the reorganization of municipal government has been much more controversial. In 1985, the state Labour government announced a plan to reduce the number of municipalities by half. The policy resulted in state-wide demonstrations and a march on the state parliament buildings.[11] The government retreated. It was replaced by a Liberal-National coalition led by Jeffrey Kennett, who had once "publicly congratulated those who had resisted amalgamations and declared that the Liberal party would continue to defend their right to be administered by the local government system of their choice."[12]

Once in office, Kennett changed direction and reduced the number of Victoria's municipalities from 210 to 78. The policy prompted court challenges, protest, and administrative chaos – but it was implemented. Vince's conclusion about the recent experience in Victoria is that the process

> ...highlights the tremendous complexity involved in boundary changes and organisational mergers... [It] is also evidence that poorly planned, hastily executed amalgamations, which do not involve intense consultation with councillors, staff and communities of amalgamating councils, can result in long term organisational problems which adversely affect service delivery.[13]

Another assessment of the Victoria amalgamations comes from Rosemary Kiss of the Centre for Public Policy at the University of Melbourne:

> ...[T]he Kennett government continues to state that huge savings have resulted from its remaking of the municipal map. Savings of up to $400mill. have been claimed. While it is very difficult to be conclusive, analysis of ABS [Australian Bureau of Statistics] figures suggests that these claims are wildly inaccurate. If we compare Victorian local government operational expenditures of $2,452,066,000 in 1991/92, the last complete year before the Kennett government was elected, with those of $2,859,031,000 for 1996/97, the latest figures available, and then inflate the 1991/92 figure to 1997 values, giving a figure of $2,746,862,000 it would seem that operating costs have actually increased. Rates [property

---

11. Vince, "Amalgamations," p.158.
12. Rosemary Kiss, "Local Government to Local Administration," in Brian Costar and Nick Economou, eds. *The Kennett Revolution: Victorian Politics in the 1990s* (Sydney: University of New South Wales Press, 1999). This article is also available by clicking on "Library" at: <http://www.localselfgovt.org>.
13. Vince, "Amalgamations," pp.159-60.

taxes] have gone down considerably... but so has capital expenditure which means that 'savings' have only been made by failing to maintain infrastructure. On matters of financial and efficiency costs and benefits of the Kennett government's changes to local government, there is still a need for much more research and analysis. Nevertheless, there are strong grounds for stating that local communities have not made any sustainable economic gains.[14]

Sydney, in the state of New South Wales, is Australia's largest city-region, with a population of 3.5 million. There has been little change in the municipal organization of the Sydney city-region in recent decades. The region comprises 45 municipalities. The most populous in 1998 was the city of Blacktown (244,176). The population of the central city of Sydney was 19,913.[15]

GREAT BRITAIN

Margaret Thatcher's period as prime minister (1979-90) brought huge changes to British local government, including mandatory tendering of contracts for the provision of local government services, the privatization of the water supply system, expenditure caps, and a poll tax. The government she led sponsored legislation that abolished the Greater London Council and six upper-tier metropolitan councils that had been established in the 1970s for the most populous city-regions. In her memoirs, she stated that prior to leaving office she had become convinced that even the upper-tier county councils needed to be abolished.[16] In short, Margaret Thatcher was no friend of big local government. There were no local government amalgamations during her prime ministership. Indeed, in 1988, the right-wing, pro-market Adam Smith Institute issued a report "advocating the establishment of a set of small unitary authorities [single tier] of around 40,000 [population], delivering most of their service on a contract basis."[17]

Under Prime Minister John Major (1990-1997), significant local government restructuring did occur outside Greater London. The main

14. Kiss, "Local Government."
15. <http://www.lsga.org.au/web.councils.nsf/Listing>
16. Margaret Thatcher, *The Downing Street Years* (New York: Harper Collins, 1993), p.663.
17. Steve Leach and Gerry Stoker, "Understanding the Local Government Review: A Retrospective Analysis," *Public Administration*, 75 (Spring 1997), 5.

issue was whether new structures should include only one tier (unitary authorities) or whether they should maintain the two-tier structure established in 1974. After great turmoil and confusion in England, the end result was that four upper-tier counties were abolished and 20 more lost territory. Within this affected territory, 46 new unitary authorities were created. Under the old system there were 296 lower-tier districts within two-tier systems; after the changes there were 238 (as well as the 46 new unitary authorities).[18] In Scotland, 28 unitary authorities replaced 12 upper-tier regional councils and 65 lower-tier councils. In Wales, 21 unitary authorities replaced eight counties and the 37 districts within them.[19] One academic commentator's assessment of these changes was the following: "There had been little rationality; goals, and the means of achieving them, were fuzzy, and clouded further by the vast and changing number of participants... The outcome could hardly be counted a Major success story."[20]

Since 1997, the government of Prime Minister Tony Blair has been concerned with creating new national legislatures for Scotland and Wales and a new upper-tier Greater London Authority, complete with Britain's first directly-elected mayor. While the old Greater London Council employed 25,000, plans for the new authority project that there will be a staff of only about 200. [21] The Blair government appears to have no plans to sponsor further municipal amalgamations.

---

18. Leach and Stoker, "Understanding," p.13.
19. John Kingdom, "Centralisation and Fragmentation: John Major and the Reform of Local Government" in Peter Dorey, ed., The Major Premiership: Politics and Policies under John Major, 1990-97 (Basingstoke, Hampshire: Macmillan, 1999), p.52.
20. Kingdom, "Centralisation," p.52.
21. Hugh Atkinson, "New Labour, New Local Government?" in Gerald R. Taylor, ed., The Impact of New Labour (Basingstoke, Hampshire, Macmillan, 1999), pp.139-40.

NOVA SCOTIA[22]

Notwithstanding a royal commission report in 1974 that called for extensive municipal amalgamations in Nova Scotia,[23] there were no legislated mergers until 1995. Indeed, in 1980, a *new* municipality – the town of Bedford – was created within the Halifax area. The current interest in municipal restructuring in Nova Scotia began in 1991, when the minister of municipal affairs created a Task Force on Local Government chaired by his deputy. The report of the task force was concerned just as much with the re-alignment of provincial and municipal responsibilities as with boundaries. Nevertheless, it did recommend the creation of new amalgamated unitary authorities within the territories of at least five of Nova Scotia's 18 counties.[24] It justified its position in these words:

> A unitary government (one-tier)... is clearly responsible for all local services in the region. Its members are thus readily accountable. The inefficiencies in multiple bodies with overlapping tasks are avoided. It is probably more economical than the combined units it replaces (certainly so if three or more units are replaced.) It is able to take a broad view of the entire range of services, the tax burden that people can bear, and the service needs of the entire community. This will lead to efficiencies in decision making, and less wastage of public funds generally.

> The recommended unitary governments will result in substantial savings for the taxpayer.[25]

Such assertions were presented as though they could not possibly be disputed. There is no evidence that anyone associated with the Task Force knew that the matter had been a subject of fierce academic debate, let alone that the academic consolidationists had effectively lost.

In late 1992, Premier Donald Cameron announced that consolidation would go ahead in both Cape Breton and Halifax. But in May 1993 he was

22. The discussion of the events relating to Halifax prior to 1 April 1996 is taken from Andrew Sancton, "Reducing Costs by Consolidating Municipalities: New Brunswick, Nova Scotia, Ontario," *Canadian Public Administration*, 39-3 (Fall 1996), 267-89.
23. Nova Scotia, Royal Commission on Education, Public Services and Provincial-Municipal Relations, *Report* (Halifax: Queen's Printer, 1974), p.5-7.
24. Nova Scotia, Task Force on Local Government, *Report to the Government of Nova Scotia*, April 1992, p.43. Counties in Nova Scotia are single-tier rural municipalities that generally surround incorporated villages, towns, and cities.
25. Nova Scotia, Task Force, *Report* (1992), pp.32-3.

replaced as premier by the former mayor of Dartmouth, John Savage, who proclaimed during the election campaign that amalgamation of the four Halifax municipalities was "a crazy idea."[26] Soon afterwards, reports were received from "implementation commissioners" outlining how mergers in Cape Breton and Halifax could take place. The one for Cape Breton stated that amalgamation of the designated municipalities would save $6.5 million per year, so that total operating expenditures in the first year of operation would be $77.1 million.[27] In mid-1994, Premier Savage announced his support for municipal consolidation in Cape Breton. It came into effect in August 1995.

The single-tier Cape Breton Regional Municipality merged one city (Sydney), six towns, and one rural municipality (the county of Cape Breton). According to the 1991 federal census, the population of this area was 120,000 or 75 per cent of the population of all of Cape Breton, 13 per cent of all Nova Scotia. Because the province significantly changed municipal functions and financial arrangements at about the same time as the merger, it is extremely difficult to assess its overall impact. It would appear, however, that its main accomplishment was to rescue at least some of the former towns from impending bankruptcy. The towns no longer exist, but residents within their former boundaries now benefit from sharing the healthy tax base of the former county, which contained relatively prosperous urbanized areas within its boundaries. Tax rates in 1998 within the boundaries of the former county were higher than pre-amalgamation levels and rates within Sydney and most of the former towns were lower.[28]

The 1993 report of the implementation commissioner for Halifax, C. William Hayward, contained a detailed financial analysis of how much money would be saved for each municipal function as a result of amalgamation of the cities of Halifax and Dartmouth, the town of Bedford, and Halifax county and the Metropolitan Authority, a weak inter-municipal agency concerned primarily with public transit, which had proven incapable of reaching a satisfactory compromise concerning the disposal of the

---

26. *The Globe & Mail*, October 28, 1994.
27. Nova Scotia, Municipal Affairs, *Interim Report of the Implementation Commissioner, Cape Breton County*, 1993.
28. I am indebted to Rick Ramsay, former CAO of King's county in Nova Scotia, for most of my knowledge of the situation in Cape Breton. Mr. Ramsay successfully completed his MPA at the University of Western Ontario by writing a research report on the merger. He contributed much of the material on Cape Breton to a manuscript on Canadian municipal mergers and intermunicipal agreements that I co-authored with Rebecca James and him for the Intergovernmental Committee on Urban and Regional Research.

area's solid waste. In the fiscal year 1992-93 Hayward estimated total spending for the four municipalities and the Authority to be $439.6 million. Savings resulting from amalgamation were stated as $9.8 million, or 2.2 per cent of the total budget. Almost half the savings ($4.4 million) were to come from "General Government Services."[29] There was no reference in the report to any academic studies about the relationship between the size of municipalities and the cost of their municipal services. Nor was there any reference to the possibility that some of the savings he documented might have been possible without amalgamation.

It would be unfair to suggest that the Hayward report paid no attention to non-financial issues. There were claims that a unitary system would be "more responsive," that "accountability... will be improved," that "planning... will also be more effective," and that "sounder financial decisions, particularly for capital spending, should also result."[30] Two pages in the report are devoted to discussing the disadvantages of a two-tier system of regional government and of a system that relies on voluntary inter-municipal co-operation.[31]

Hayward did acknowledge two potential difficulties. The first was that, "In larger municipal units citizens may view their governments as distant and inaccessible." His solution was to provide for a network of "community councils, community committees, community advisory committees and citizen advisory committees."[32] He briefly discussed the Winnipeg experience with such bodies, listing seven different reasons why they had not worked. He then pointed out that these kinds of committees had been tried in Halifax county and in Cape Breton, without making any judgement concerning their effectiveness. He concluded the discussion by writing:

> The intention is to provide a way for citizens to have a greater say in the way services are provided, in what services are provided, and in the form the community will take. At the same time, whatever advantages can be obtained from a larger unit are kept. The result should be accessible and responsive government at the least cost.[33]

The second problem was the new municipality's sheer territorial size, especially the difficulties posed by the existence of a very large, sparsely

---

29. Nova Scotia, Municipal Affairs, *Interim Report of the Municipal Reform Commissioner, Halifax County (Halifax Metropolitan Area)*, 1993, p.75.
30. Nova Scotia, *Interim Report, Halifax*, 1993, p.38.
31. Nova Scotia, *Interim Report, Halifax*, 1993, pp.39-41.
32. Nova Scotia, *Interim Report, Halifax*, 1993, p.43.
33. Nova Scotia, *Interim Report, Halifax*, 1993, p.46.

populated rural hinterland in Halifax county. Here Hayward made a telling admission:

> Those who look simply at numbers and conclude that the rural areas will be out-voted and ignored are overlooking the way the democratic process works. Councillors, like any other elected persons (absent party discipline), will support the concerns of others in an attempt to generate support for their own pet projects.[34]

Hayward seemed to have no idea that this particular defence of his favoured scheme is often cited by "public choice" analysts as a major reason why large governmental units are inherently wasteful.[35] The problem is precisely as Hayward outlined it. If councillors have a pet project that they support above all else, they will support the pet projects of others in order to make sure that they support them. The end result is that more projects are actually approved than "the median voter" would desire. This is much more likely to happen in larger units than in smaller ones because, in smaller ones, there is more likelihood that councillors will share a common interest in all proposed projects. As an accountant, Hayward saw opportunities in amalgamation for savings. As a political analyst he appeared to be justifying his proposal with an argument that inevitably would lead to increased expenditure.

Despite Premier Savage's initial declared opposition to amalgamation, he reversed his position in October 1994 as part of an overall strategy to reduce government spending and promote economic development. He also claimed that squabbling among the Halifax area municipalities had become worse since he had become premier. The government's new policy caused the four affected municipalities to sponsor their own consultants' studies of the proposed amalgamation. The consultants' report generally accepted Hayward's findings about cost savings[36] but pointed out that they would roughly be cancelled out by increases in expenditures caused by "policy harmonization" and "service levelling."[37] The consultants also questioned Hayward"s support for community councils:

---

34. Nova Scotia, *Interim Report, Halifax*, 1993, pp.47-8.
35. See Gordon Tullock, *The New Federalist, adapted for Canadian readers by Filip Palda* (Vancouver: The Fraser Institute, 1994) pp.55-9.
36. UMA Group in Association with Doane Raymond, *Analysis of Municipal Amalgamation*, prepared for The City of Halifax, The City of Dartmouth, The Town of Bedford and Halifax County Municipality, 12 April 1995, p.34.
37. UMA Group, *Municipal Amalgamation*, 1995, pp. i & 31-3.

> [W]e have some concerns about the need and benefit of community councils. These councils evolved in urban areas of Halifax County. Does the need still exist for Community Councils when these areas become part of a municipal government that is urban dominated? In our opinion, the Community Councils are not required.[38]

The consultants did, however, end up supporting the unitary approach. They acknowledged that "the greatest concern is this new municipal government may become far too removed from the people that it governs."[39] Only through administrative decentralization and "customer-oriented" delivery systems could this problem be overcome. In order to take account of the special concerns of rural residents, the consultants recommended that their wards have only one quarter as many people in them as urban wards.[40]

By May 1995 the legislation establishing the Halifax Regional Municipality was approved. There was relatively little difficulty in the legislature because the official opposition, the Conservatives, were the ones who had launched the amalgamation plans in the first place. The legislation included provisions for community councils. There was no special representation for rural areas on the 24-member council. In December, elections were held for the new council and on 1 April 1996 the new municipality took over from the four old ones and from the Metropolitan Authority. Halifax Regional Municipality (HRM) has a population of 354,000, 37.5 per cent of the Nova Scotia total. Its territory is 5,577 square kilometres (compared to 5,660 square kilometres for all of Prince Edward Island) or 10.6 per cent of Nova Scotia's land area. It is so big that the census metropolitan area of Halifax, as defined by Statistics Canada, covers only half its territory, the half that contains 95 per cent of HRM's population.[41]

Comprehensive assessments of HRM's performance have not yet been completed.[42] Clearly, however, the transition period is over. It was a success

---

38. UMA Group, *Municipal Amalgamation*, 1995, p.57.
39. UMA Group, *Municipal Amalgamation*, 1995, p.58.
40. UMA Group, *Municipal Amalgamation*, 1995, p.61.
41. Halifax Regional Municipality, *HRM Access and Information Guide*, no date.
42. I am a member of the national research team for the Halifax Amalgamation Project, funded by the Donner Foundation and based at the School of Public Administration, Dalhousie University. What follows does not necessarily represent the views of anyone else associated with the project and is based on information already in the public domain. For information on the project see <http://www.mgmt.dal.ca/spa> and click "research."

only in the sense that HRM survived. By all other conceivable measures, it was disastrous.[43] William Hayward was appointed by the government to oversee the transition. One of his most important functions was to appoint the HRM's first chief administrative officer (CAO). He chose Ken Meech, the county's CAO. A year later, Mr. Meech co-authored a remarkably candid account of how he experienced the transition. His first comment was that the transition was too rushed. He was hired only five months before the amalgamation came into effect and the new council took office only three months before. Mr. Meech believed that the CAO should have been hired by the new council, not by Mr. Hayward.[44]

Mr. Meech made the following observation about how HRM's financial situation went wrong from the very beginning:

> Prior to the amalgamation, each of the former municipalities initiated capital projects that would not have been pursued under normal circumstances. This depleted their financial reserves. To make matters worse, 3 of the 4 had deficits in their final year of operations... Before any amalgamation occurs, criteria for spending, hiring, and long-term contracting should be established and strictly enforced in order to regulate the activities of the subject municipalities. The goal is to protect the interests of the new municipality from the announcement of the amalgamation until its completion.[45]

---

43. Newspaper accounts of the process are numerous. See, for example, "Halifax merger falls short of hopes," *The London Free Press*, 12 November 1996; "Halifax-Dartmouth's amalgamation has been a case study in Murphy's law: If it could go wrong it did," *Saint John Times-Globe*, 21 November 1996; "Halifax shows us how not to amalgamate: Forced creation of a supercity has raised costs and cut services," *Toronto Star*, 8 December 1996; "Bigger not better: Halifax supercity's had a rough first year and wage costs may make 1997 worse," *Hamilton Spectator*, 6 February 1997.

44. Ken R. Meech and Rudy Vodicka, "Hindsight is 20/20: Planning for Amalgamation in the Halifax Regional Municipality," *Cordillera Institute Journal*, 1-1(1997), 10.

45. Meech and Vodicka, "Hindsight," p.10. That action be taken at the time of the announcement of the government's policy for amalgamation was exactly what was done by the Government of Ontario with respect to amalgamation in Toronto. But the courts ruled that, under Ontario law, the government had no such authority. See Mr. Justice Brennan's judgment in Ontario Court of Justice, *Corporation of the City of Scarborough v. Attorney General for Ontario*, 24 February 1997 <http://community.web.net/citizens/103Updates/feb24.html>.

Other comments from Mr. Meech follow:

> One of the most elusive challenges we face is the merging of the different organizational cultures. Staff resistance to cultural change was and is a major cause of internal conflict at all levels...
>
> A major cause of public, council, and staff discontent associated with amalgamation is the failure to meet expectations...
>
> For example, a common public expectation is that amalgamation reduces staff numbers (which, in turn, yields cost savings) while maintaining services at levels similar to or better than those before amalgamation. Yet, almost the opposite happened at HRM. For example, dramatic staff reductions occurred in Finance despite the fact that some of the most profound operational changes were to be made in that department. As a result, its staffing levels were found wanting. This, in turn, drove up costs in the short run as more consultants, more overtime, and more part-time staff were needed to develop minimal financial operations. As might be expected, service delivery challenges resulted...
>
> HRM has inherited 31 collective bargaining agreements. While the ultimate objective is to reduce that number to 5, we currently find ourselves mired in the past, trying to patch differences among the various agreements, when we should be attempting to reach common operational provisions...[46]

Mr. Meech's example of driving up costs "in the short run" was multiplied many times over. Problems with computer and communications systems were particularly difficult.[47] Mr. Hayward had estimated transition costs at $10 million. The final figure was $26 million. HRM received no provincial financial assistance for these costs, but it was allowed to borrow to cover them. Servicing the transition debt cost $2.3 million in 1998.[48]

Notwithstanding the creation of the HRM, its arrangements for governance and taxation remain quite complex. There are three distinct areas for property taxation purposes – core, suburban, and rural – each with its own rate for different classes of property. Boundaries for these areas are decided by the HRM council on the basis of the level of services provided in different places. There are five community councils that group council members from adjoining electoral districts (wards). The areas covered by community councils do not correspond to the boundaries of the

---

46. Meech and Vodicka, "Hindsight," pp.11-2
47. For details, see Igor Vojnovic, *Municipal Consolidation in the 1990s: An Analysis of Five Canadian Municipalities* (Toronto: ICURR Press, 1997), pp.89-110.
48. *Halifax Chronicle-Herald*, 2 October 1998.

old municipalities, to the core-suburban-rural boundaries for taxation purposes, nor to the boundaries of planning advisory committees established under the provincial planning legislation. Although most of their functions are advisory to the HRM council, the community councils do have the authority to amend land-use by-laws and enter into development agreements with respect to land within their communities, as long as such decisions are consistent with HRM planning strategy.[49] Since some of the councils have as few as three members and since media attention is limited at best, there are concerns about openness and transparency with respect to land-use planning. The council member for downtown Halifax – who refuses to participate in the community councils – believes that they have too much power and that they make the system more complex than it was before amalgamation. Other councillors consider that they work quite well.[50]

Probably the HRM's greatest accomplishment has been to resolve the long-standing inter-municipal disputes about solid-waste disposal. HRM now has an elaborate waste-separation system, a new landfill site, and a state-of-the art composting facility. The main reported problems stem from the fact that many residents of the outlying areas of HRM seem to resent having to participate in a system that they feel has been designed for big-city environmentalists. Without extensive further research, it is impossible to determine whether the resolution of this issue can be credited directly to the amalgamation. The obvious point to remember is that other city-regions solve solid-waste problems without a comprehensive amalgamation.

Another success story has been the improvement in the quality of Dartmouth's water supply. Prior to amalgamation there were real difficulties, including occasional periods when residents had to boil water prior to drinking it. The city of Halifax refused to sell water to Dartmouth. After amalgamation, the systems were integrated.

There is no question that prior to amalgamation, relations between the cities of Halifax and Dartmouth were badly strained. Part of the problem might have stemmed from the royal commission recommendation in 1974 that they be merged, a threat revived in 1992 by the task force on local government. Whenever there is the threat of outside intervention to amend structural arrangements, it is usually in the interest of a perceived beneficiary not to co-operate in arriving at long-term negotiated solutions to

49. Eudora Pendergrast and John Farrow, *Community Councils and Neighbour-hood Committees: Lessons for our Communities from around the World* (Toronto: Canadian Urban Institute, 1997), Appendix A-2, pp.2-3.
50. Halifax This Week:
<http://novanewsnet.ukings.ns.ca/stories/96-97/970314/amalgamation.htm>

outstanding irritants. A more immediate and obvious source of discord, however, was the intense competition between Dartmouth and Halifax to market land in their respective industrial parks.[51] The two cities were apparently unrestricted by provincial legislation in their competitive quest to sell land cheaply. The spectacle of each municipality trying to outdo the other by virtually giving away land whose development had been subsidized by the provincial and federal governments was unacceptable to many Haligonians, especially ones who happened to be federal or provincial politicians. It was also unacceptable to the Halifax Board of Trade, many of whose members were presumably owners of industrial land, the value of which was being eroded. In any event, the Board of Trade (now the Metropolitan Halifax Chamber of Commerce) was an early proponent of amalgamation on the grounds that it would aid economic development by eliminating inter-municipal competition.

The HRM has indeed stopped competition in land sales in municipal industrial parks. This is probably good public policy and it is certainly in the interests of industrial landowners. How it will help attract new investors to the Halifax area is far from clear.[52] A business-municipal partnership for the marketing of Halifax was created shortly before amalgamation. Its apparent success has no doubt been assisted by the absence of inter-municipal squabbling. It is difficult, however, to point to obvious success stories. The Greater Halifax Partnership claims to have brought 36 new companies to Halifax since its creation.

The partnership's general manager points with pride to the recent decision of a large American company to employ 300 people at a newly established call centre in Sackville, a small suburban community previously part of Halifax county. In a recent interview with *Le Soleil* he is quoted as saying:

> Jamais cette compagnie n'aurait pensé de s'établir à cet endroit si la région n'avait pas été fusionnée. Jamais elle n'aurait entendu parler de

---

51. Hugh Millward and Shelley Dickey, "Industrial Decentralization and the Planned Industrial Park: A Case Study of Metropolitan Halifax" in Frances Frisken, ed., *The Changing Canadian Metropolis: A Public Policy Perspective* (Berkeley CA: Institute of Governmental Studies Press at the University of California, 1994), pp.751-76.

52. An American study of 129 large metropolitan areas found no apparent link between municipal structural arrangements and levels of economic growth. See Kathryn A. Foster, "Exploring the Links Between Political Structure and Economic Growth," *Political Geography*, 12-6 (1993), 523-47.

Sackville. Mais elle connaissait Halifax, une grande ville qui compte maintenant 350,000 habitants.[53]

This is an exceptionally curious line of argument. We are expected to believe that it was municipal amalgamation that made the difference, not the existence of a marketing agency acting on behalf of the entire area. Many city-regions have the latter; very few are amalgamated into one municipality. What possible difference could it have made to the investor whether or not the former municipalities were amalgamated?

Ironically, much of the motivation to market Halifax more effectively was spurred by the perceived success of Moncton, New Brunswick, a small city-region containing three significant municipalities – Moncton, Dieppe, and Riverview – that were deliberately *not* merged because a 1994 provincial panel reported as follows:

> When one considers... that it is only at the municipal level that Acadians can hold majority political power in New Brunswick, it is easier to understand the strong negative reaction of the residents of Dieppe and many Francophones in the general area to the prospect of amalgamation.[54]

Three years after the HRM's creation there is nobody who believes that William Hayward's original projections about saving money have come to pass. After visiting Halifax recently, Julie Lemieux of *Le Soleil* reported that "L'instigateur de ces attentes démesurées s'appelle Bill Hayward. La simple évocation de son nom donne des frissons aux élus, comme aux employés municipaux, au public comme aux gens d'affaires."[55] Nevertheless, at this stage it is exceptionally difficult to untangle the official financial record. There are two main problems: 1) year-over-year total municipal expenditures are of little use for this period because, simultaneous with the amalgamation, the province implemented "service exchange," whereby

---

53. Michael MacDonald, as quoted in Julie Lemieux, "Fusions municipales: Surtout pas une question d'économie," *Le Soleil*, 28 October 1999.

54. J.E. Louis Malenfant and John C. Robison, *Greater Moncton Urban community: Strength through Cooperation* (Fredericton: Ministry of Municipalities, Culture and Housing, 1994), p.34. As a result of the work of a similar panel, the city of Miramichi (population 21,600) was created in 1995 by merging the cities of Chatham, Newcastle, three villages and surrounding areas. See John C. Robison, "Public Participation in Restructuring Local Government to Create the City of Miramichi" in K.A. Graham and S.D. Phillips, eds., Citizen Engagement: Lessons in Participation from Local Government (Toronto: Institute of Public Administration of Canada, 1998), pp.188-99.

55. "La fusion d'Halifax: de vaines promesses...," 28 October 1999.

provincial-municipal responsibilities, especially for welfare and roads, were significantly altered; and 2) even, if one looks at a department not affected by service exchange – such as fire – the financial records of HRM, in its early months at least, are so confused and inconsistent that there is no way of knowing whether or not these records are accounting for the same activities over different periods of time. For example, sometimes the fire department's expenses seem to include costs for information systems, sometimes they do not. For individual taxpayers, the situation is even more confusing because new and significant property assessments were also introduced at the same time as amalgamation.

One point, however, is fairly clear. Had service exchange gone ahead without amalgamation, taxpayers in Halifax county – where, relative to the rest of the region, there are more kilometres of roads and fewer welfare recipients – would have been hit with significant tax increases. One of the main fiscal effects of the amalgamation was the use of what would have been a windfall gain for taxpayers in the city of Halifax to cushion the negative impact on county taxpayers.[56] Ironically, then, if we accept that service exchange was going to happen anyway, we can conclude that amalgamation, by limiting tax increases in the former county area, will have the effect of facilitating suburban development and making it relatively more expensive to live in the central city. In theory, of course, HRM could place tough limits on suburban development, but there is no evidence that this is happening.

The implications of harmonized collective agreements for HRM workers have not yet been properly documented. At one stage or another since amalgamation, HRM has experienced strikes or work slowdowns by virtually all its unionized employees. HRM's mayor, Walter Fitzgerald, former mayor of the city of Halifax, is obviously upset with the whole process: "Évidemment, personne n'a voulu ajuster son salaire à la baisse. Tout le monde a voulu niveler vers le haut... Si Dartmouth n'avait pas aussi bien payé ses employés, ça nous aurait coûté beaucoup moins cher."[57]

Concerning levels of service, it appears that some services in rural areas have been improved, notably support for recreation programs and volunteer fire departments. The long-term concern, however, is that HRM involvement will erode long traditions of rural voluntarism. An HRM citizen survey in 1997 showed that most citizens were satisfied with municipal

56.Dale H. Poel and Ruth Bruer, "The Consequences of Amalgamation: Setting the Research Agenda for the HRM Project," paper presented to the CAPPA/IPAC annual conference, Montreal, August 1998, p.10.
57.As quoted in Julie Lemieux, "La fusion d'Halifax,"

services, even though a majority in each of the areas of the five community councils was still opposed to amalgamation.[58] A 1999 survey of residents conducted by the HRM Amalgamation Project at Dalhousie University showed that for eight out of nine different municipal services, more respondents thought services were worse after amalgamation than before. The most harshly judged service was street and road paving and repair; 49 per cent thought this was worse, only 6 per cent that it was better. The one service that was judged favourably was refuse, recycling, organics collection; 21 per cent thought that it was worse, 47 per cent that it was better.[59] The same survey showed that, three years after amalgamation, 66 per cent of respondents were either "opposed" or "strongly opposed" to the amalgamation (the figure for "strongly opposed" being 39 per cent).[60]

Julie Lemieux begins her comprehensive account of the Halifax amalgamation by writing: "Les gens d'affaires applaudissent, les contribuables grognent, et les élus patinent."[61] Such an assessment sums up the situation remarkably well. The most fervent defenders of amalgamation are clearly within the Greater Halifax Partnership and the Halifax chamber of commerce. Lemieux quotes the chamber's president as saying:

> Pour nous, la fusion des municipalités a été très positive, peu importe ce que les citoyens peuvent en dire. Nous avons une voix plus forte dans le monde entier pour vendre nos produits et nous n'envoyons plus de messages contradictoires. Et maintenant que les difficultés qu'a entraînées la fusion font partie du passé, ça ne peut que s'améliorer. Déjà, les gens regardent l'avenir avec plus d'optimisme.[62]

This is the last redoubt of the proponents of amalgamation: it is better to have one municipality selling Halifax than four – a proposition that can only be accepted on faith alone.

There is still much to be discovered about the reasons for, and results of, the Halifax amalgamation. Why did Premier John Savage, a former mayor of Dartmouth, change his position on this issue? Did he and his

---

58. Halifax Regional Municipality, "1997 Citizen Survey Results."
59. Dale H. Poel, "[Not] Thinking Regionally: Citizen Responses to Municipal Consolidation," a paper presented at the annual meeting of the Canadian Regional Science Association, Montreal, November 1999, p.7.
60. Poel, "[Not] Thinking Regionally," p.3.
61. "Surtout pas une question d'éonomie," Le Soleil, 28 October 1999.
62. Peter Doig, as quoted in Julie Lemieux, "Fusions municipales à Halifax: Coup de pouce à la croissance économique," Le Soleil, 29 October 1999.

cabinet colleagues fully understand at the time that amalgamation would ease the differential outcomes for property tax levels in city and county resulting from service exchange? Did they really believe that one municipality could better promote economic growth? If so, what evidence did they have? Or did they rely on assertions from the chamber of commerce? Why were chamber members so concerned about inter-municipal competition in the selling of municipally owned industrial land? Will the financial records of HRM ever be sufficiently untangled so that researchers will be able to compare pre- and post-amalgamation costs? Only when such questions can be answered will anybody be able with confidence to tell the complete story of the Halifax amalgamation. Until then we can conclude only that events in Halifax over the past four years give little comfort to those who favour comprehensive municipal consolidations.

Ontario

The best-known municipal amalgamation in Ontario in the 1990s was the megacity created in Toronto in 1998. It will be discussed in the next chapter. Here the subjects are the significant amalgamations sponsored by previous Liberal and NDP governments and by the non-Toronto amalgamations implemented by the Harris Conservatives.

The past decade of tumultuous change for Ontario's municipal government began innocently enough in 1989 when an advisory committee to the Liberal minister of municipal affairs stated that, "In principle, local municipal corporations should be consolidated to have a minimum population of 4,000."[63] The recommendation was so controversial that the minister soon backed away: "... 4,000 in many instances would be too small to encompass a natural service area or provide an adequate financial base for the services demanded, just as it would be unnecessarily large or inappropriate in several others."[64] In 1990, the Liberals settled a long-simmering boundary dispute around Sarnia by allowing the city to absorb all of the neighbouring town of Clearwater, while simultaneously providing for the new city of Sarnia to become a member of Lambton county council. Despite having 58 per cent of the new county's population of 120,000, the

63. Ontario, Municipal Affairs, *Consultation Committee to the Minister, County Government in Ontario,* (January 1989), p.22.
64. Ontario, Municipal Affairs, *Toward an Ideal County* (January 1990), p.2.

city was allocated only 15 of 37 county council votes.[65] In south Simcoe county, northwest of Toronto, the Liberals sponsored legislation to force the consolidation of eight lower-tier municipalities into three. In all the various studies relating to south Simcoe[66] there was little or no reference to saving money or reducing the number of politicians. The emphasis was on creating municipalities that would be capable of servicing new urban development in a planned and orderly fashion. In the late 1980s this was an area subject to strong pressures for growth. Honda had located a new automobile assembly plant in Alliston, and Toronto commuters found the area cheaper to live in than more proximate suburbs.

When the NDP came to office in late 1990, there was little change in provincial policies relating to municipal amalgamation. The NDP introduced legislation in 1993 to consolidate municipalities in north Simcoe. During the debate, Jim Wilson, the Conservative member for the area and later a prominent cabinet minister in the Harris government stated:

> I've spent the last several months reviewing all the regional governments in Ontario, many of which were imposed by my party in the past, so believe me, I come to this with some experience, and the south Simcoe experience to date. There are no cost savings. Bigger is not better. The government cannot point to an area of this province, including south Simcoe, where amalgamating departments has resulted in savings to the ratepayer. It does not exist. In fact, history shows that smaller units are more efficient...
>
> I to this day cannot find anyone in Tottenham, Beeton, Alliston or Tecumseth township who liked restructuring. They do not like it, including a number of people on council. We've had all kinds of problems...[67]

The NDP also sponsored legislation tripling the area of London.[68] The town of Westminster to the south was completely absorbed into London, as

---

65.Byron J. Montgomery, *Annexation and Restructuring in Sarnia-Lambton: A Model for Ontario County Government?* Local Government Case Studies #4 (London, Ontario: University of Western Ontario Department of Political Science, 1991), p.71.

66.For a summary, see Allan O'Brien, *Municipal Consolidation in Canada and its Alternatives* (Toronto: ICURR Publications, 1993), pp.78-81.

67.Ontario, Legislative Assembly, *Hansard*, Standing Committee on Social Development, August 23, 1993, pp. S-181-2.

68.For more details, see Andrew Sancton, "Negotiating, Arbitrating, Legislating: Where was the Public in London's Boundary Adjustment?" in Graham and Phillips, eds., *Citizen Engagement*, pp.163-87.

were portions of adjoining townships to the north, east, and west. This amalgamation was significant for two reasons. First, the provincial position – during the deep recession of the early 1990s – was that amalgamation was necessary to promote economic development in the area and the province as a whole. Westminster was at the junction of highways 401 and 402, considered a prime spot for future industrial growth. But Westminster did not have the financial resources to build the necessary infrastructure; therefore, according to the province, London needed to take over. Seven years after the amalgamation there has been no new industrial development around the intersection of the two highways. Indeed, piped infrastructure is still not in place, presumably because there is no demand.

The second significant feature of the London amalgamation was that the NDP minister of municipal affairs eventually decided to settle the dispute between London and its neighbours by appointing an "arbitrator" with strict terms of reference, and promising to implement what the arbitrator decided. Such a practice was later adopted by the Harris Conservatives, except that the position was styled as "commissioner" or "special advisor," depending on the legal authority vested in the individual in question. One of the many curious features of the London amalgamation was that the arbitrator had little alternative under his terms of reference except to allocate to the city far more new territory than it had originally requested. When in opposition as the legislature's "third party," most of the Harris Conservatives in October 1992 voted against the legislation implementing the arbitrator's decision, although the local Conservative member for London North, Dianne Cunningham (also a future Harris cabinet minister), voted in favour.

Speaking in Fergus, Ontario, in the autumn of 1994, only a few months before the election that brought him to power, Mike Harris himself clearly articulated the position that his party had taken with respect to municipal amalgamations in London and north Simcoe:

> There is no cost to a municipality to maintain its name and identity. Why destroy our roots and pride? I disagree with restructuring because it believes that bigger is better. Services always cost more in larger communities. The issue is to find out how to distribute services fairly and equally without duplicating services.[69]

---

69. As quoted by John Barber in "Harris's words come back to bite him," *The Globe and Mail*, February 19, 1997.

103

This position was totally consistent with the provisions of the *Common Sense Revolution* (CSR), his party's carefully crafted election platform. Its only reference to municipal structures was that "regional and municipal levels" of government should be "rationalize[d]... to avoid overlap and duplication that now exists."[70]

Two months after becoming premier, Mr. Harris addressed the annual meeting of the Association of Municipalities of Ontario (AMO). He made no reference to the need for any form of municipal restructuring.[71] The new minister of municipal affairs and housing, Al Leach, addressed the same conference the day before. He made one reference to municipal amalgamation:

> There is no solution that's going to work everywhere. But there are a lot of measures that can make a difference: successful amalgamations, for example – like the one that created the Town of New Tecumseth; there's annexations, sharing services, deciding what services should be provided; there's the cost management approach used so well by Pittsburgh Township; and there's government restructuring.
>
> I want to say I am fully committed to getting the province off your back.[72]

The reference to New Tecumseth was not accidental. To coincide with the AMO meeting, Mr. Leach published a flashy pamphlet (complete with his own picture) reporting on the results of an internal ministry study that purported to demonstrate cost savings from the amalgamation. Prominently displayed in the pamphlet, under the heading "Less Government," was the statement that the total number of municipal councillors had been reduced from 22 to nine.[73]

New Tecumseth is in south Simcoe county. It was brought into existence by amalgamation legislation sponsored by the Liberals. We have seen that the local Conservative member, Jim Wilson, considered it bad public policy. By the time of Mr. Leach's speech, Mr. Wilson was minister of health. If the party had been opposed to amalgamations and if there was no reference to them in the CSR, why was Mr. Leach touting them – just as his

---

70. Progressive Conservative Party of Ontario, *The Common Sense Revolution* (Toronto, 1994).
71. The text of the speech can be found at <gopher://govonca.gov.on.ca:70/00/po/speech/premamo2>
72. < gopher://govonca.gov.on.ca:70/00/po/speech/eamo>
73. I discussed the study and the pamphlet in more detail in "Reducing Costs by Consolidating Municipalities," *Canadian Public Administration*, 39-3 (Autumn 1996), 278-80.

predecessors from other parties had been – within a few weeks of his appointment to office? One possible answer is that officials in the ministry convinced him that the CSR could best be implemented in his portfolio through a policy of municipal amalgamations. Since they had already conducted a study showing that New Tecumseth saved money, and since it indisputably involved fewer local politicians, it could not have been difficult to convert municipal amalgamation – a long-standing objective of the ministry since the 1960s – into a policy that was consistent with the CSR call for less government.

Municipal amalgamations did not clearly appear on the Harris government's public agenda until 29 November 1995, the day on which Bill 26, the *Savings and Restructuring Act*, was first made public. Schedule M of Bill 26 defined municipal restructuring in terms of various forms of annexation and amalgamation (and separation of a municipality from a county); established a procedure for municipalities to arrive at locally agreed restructuring arrangements; and provided for the appointment, in the case of local disagreement, of a commission which would itself have the power to impose new boundaries and structures within the affected area. In his book *Promised Land: Inside the Mike Harris Revolution*, John Ibbitson states that for Tony Clement (now Harris's minister of the environment and minister of municipal affairs), "It quickly became clear… that the government had been shafted by the bureaucrats. 'The bureaucracy tended to put in every item that had been on the shelf for the past five years… It was almost like a wish list.'"[74]

Certainly the provisions concerning municipal amalgamation seem much more similar to what one would expect from the ministry's wish list rather than from Conservative MPPs and the formulators of the CSR. The notion of having local restructuring disputes settled by a commissioner with binding authority seems to have emerged from the NDP's experience in settling the long-standing annexation dispute in London.

The CSR emphasized concerns about too many "levels" of government, and made special reference to concerns about overlap between "regional and municipal" governments. Significantly, however, the municipal restructuring provisions of Bill 26 specifically excluded any part of the province covered by a two-tier metropolitan (Toronto), regional, or district (Muskoka) government. On various occasions Al Leach tried to explain this aspect of the bill. Two examples follow:

74.Toronto: Prentice Hall, 1997, p.145.

I should point out that regions and the restructured Oxford county are not included in the new process. This is because many regions are already actively involved in their own restructuring process and some, such as Ottawa-Carleton, recently completed the job of restructuring. Oxford county has done that as well, and that is why it is excluded from the new legislation.[75]

There have been no major municipal boundary changes within Ottawa-Carleton and Oxford for many years. It was not clear what Mr. Leach meant by restructuring. What had happened in Ottawa-Carleton was that the NDP had legislated the direct election of regional councillors. It had reinforced the separation between the two levels of municipal government, which seemed to be exactly what the authors of the CSR were concerned about.

A few days later Mr. Leach said:

The structure of municipalities in Ontario today has an origin which dates back to the 1840s. While some municipalities have reformed in the context of regional governments, the structures of others are badly outdated and inefficient. Some of these municipalities might want to look at restructuring as a means of managing with less money.[76]

Here the argument seemed to be that because regional governments are themselves "reformed" institutions, they need not be subject to further restructuring under the terms of Bill 26. Again, such a message, if indeed it represented what the minister wanted to say, seemed in direct conflict with the terms of the CSR.

By early April 1997, more than a year after the Bill 26 procedures had been in place, there had been relatively little action with respect to municipal restructuring. The minister had approved 21 plans which, in total, had reduced the number of municipalities by 50 (out of a total of 815).[77] After this time, the pace of municipal submissions quickened. This was no doubt due to two important developments: 1) the government had, in December 1996, announced its intention to legislate the merger of all the municipalities within Metropolitan Toronto; and 2) at the end of April 1997 the first commission appointed under Bill 26 ordered the amalgamation of the city of Chatham with all municipalities within Kent county. While Mr.

---

75. Ontario, Hansard, 7 December 1995 (debate on second reading of the *Savings and Restructuring Act, 1995*).

76. Ontario, *Hansard*, Standing Committee on General Government, 18 December 1995 (hearings on the *Savings and Restructuring Act, 1995*).

77. <http://www.mmah.gov.on.ca/inthnews/releases/9704032e.htm>

Leach could claim that Toronto was a special case and that the request for a commission had come from politicians within Kent county, many municipal leaders outside these areas considered these two developments as clear evidence that if they did not restructure themselves, the government would do it for them. Many of the subsequent restructuring plans were carried out under a form of perceived duress.

The Chatham-Kent case deserves attention, not just for its influence on subsequent municipal behaviour, but also because it has been the most dramatic and extensive of all the restructurings carried out under the provisions of Bill 26. From April 1996 until January 1997, local politicians in Kent county – located halfway between London and Windsor in southwestern Ontario – had debated every conceivable alternative form of structure, from abolishing the county to merging all county municipalities into one. The only option that failed to win any degree of support was the idea that a complete merger should include the city of Chatham. On 22 January 1997, a deputy reeve died of a heart attack on the floor of the county council while defending the county's continued existence. A week later a majority of members boycotted the next meeting, which was the last opportunity to arrive at a local decision. Seven municipalities had already asked for a commission to be appointed but Mr. Leach had postponed action until it was clear that local agreement was not possible.

When he appointed a one-man commission on 6 February 1997, Mr. Leach prescribed that the area in question include both the city (population 43,000) and the county (66,000).[78] This was probably the single most important decision in the entire process – and it was clearly taken by the government, not the commissioner. After issuing an initial report in which he had narrowed the choices to either a two-tier system including the city or a one-tier system including the city, the commissioner, Peter Meyboom, reported on 28 April that he had chosen the one-tier option. He acknowledged that only one of the 23 affected municipalities, the Township of Tilbury East, supported his choice.[79]

The commissioner's decision sparked predictable statements of outrage from various municipal politicians – but after a few days the storm passed. Part of the explanation for this is that both politicians and administrators realized they would soon be jockeying for position in the new structure and no one wanted to diminish their chances by arguing that it was illegitimate.

---

78. <http://www.mmah.gov.on.ca/inthnews/releases/970206e.htm>
79. Ontario, Ministry of Municipal Affairs, County of Kent and City of Chatham Restructuring Commission, *Final Restructuring Proposal for Kent County and the City of Chatham and Order of the Commission*, 28 April 1997, p.3.

Another reason is that the Toronto megacity battle was going on at the same time and, in comparison, Chatham-Kent seemed insignificant. But, unlike Toronto, amalgamation in Chatham-Kent did not require an act of the legislature; it merged entities (the city and the county) that were not previously linked for local government purposes; and it included a city, a large town (Wallaceburg, with a population of 12,000), and various less populous towns, villages, and rural townships.

The real lesson from Chatham-Kent is that amalgamation was accepted, even though it was not popular. Residents demonstrated remarkably little public concern about the loss of their local governments as a result of one person's decision. It was as though people in the area felt that they deserved a form of punishment or strong medicine because their municipalities had behaved badly by not restructuring themselves before a commissioner was brought in. Remarkably, the government's claims that the appointment of a commissioner was a response to local wishes and that it was not responsible for the content of his decision seem to have been accepted. The fact remains, however, that never before in Ontario (or in any other liberal-democratic jurisdiction it seems) has one person had the authority – and used it – to so dramatically alter an established system of local government.

From April 1997 onward, Chatham-Kent became the horrible example that no one else wanted to follow. Counties scurried to get on with restructuring so that they would avoid a commissioner. For many, the main object was to devise a plan that would not involve becoming linked with a populous urban centre whose residents could dominate the local political process. Ironically, if all the parties involved were convinced that no one in their group would request a commissioner, the urgency to take action was greatly reduced. This probably explains why some areas acted and others did not.

Prior to the passage of Bill 26 there were 815 municipalities in Ontario. Except for the creation of the megacity in Toronto, all of the municipal restructurings approved by the Harris government prior to 1999 had been brought about under the provisions of Bill 26. As of 23 August 1999, the Harris Conservatives had caused the number of municipalities in Ontario to be reduced by 229 (28 per cent) and the number of elected municipal officials by 1,059 (23 per cent). Some of the amalgamations were clearly defensive: assessment-rich townships merged with each other so that they could avoid pressure to share their assessment with poorer neighbours. This explains why there is already talk in ministry circles of the need for "re-restructurings." The general pattern, however, has been that villages or towns have merged with neighbouring townships, despite long-standing local views that they were best kept separate due to significantly different needs for municipal services. The basic trade-off has been that the village or town shares its richer tax base in return for political dominance (through representation by population on the new council) and for new room for urban expansion.[80]

Except for Chatham, Kingston, Belleville, Peterborough and Trenton, no other Ontario cities have been affected by Bill 26. Second to Chatham, the changes in Trenton were the most dramatic. The city absorbed a village and two townships, one in a different county. That – in a sense – was the good news for Trenton. The bad news is that the city of Trenton no longer exists. Its new name is Quinte West.[81] The fact that this was the only restructuring that crossed a county boundary is important. For decades there have been complaints that county boundaries no longer matched patterns of settlement and needed to be changed. Yet, under Bill 26, the counties were the entities within which local support for restructuring was supposed to be mobilized. Quinte West was able to expand westward into Northumberland only because the Northumberland county council agreed. In other areas close to county borders (Ernestown in Lennox & Addington but closely tied to Kingston and southern Huron county abutting Grand Bend in Lambton county), inter-county agreement was not possible and restructurings were approved even though county boundaries still bisected urban areas that were otherwise part of the same urban fabric.[82]

Notwithstanding its inability to expand beyond county boundaries, the city of Kingston amalgamated with two neighbouring townships (so that its population became 120,000), including Pittsburgh, the one held up by Mr. Leach in 1995 as being a model for municipal cost containment. Belleville absorbed an entire neighbouring township,[83] and Peterborough parts of two.[84] One of the many complications in Kingston was that Pittsburgh township was not unionized. The Harris government had to introduce

80.<http://www.mmah.gov.on.ca/inthnews/releases/19990823-4e.htm> For a full discussion of the process of municipal restructuring in three rural Ontario counties, see Robert J. Williams and Terrence J. Downey, "Reforming Rural Ontario," *Canadian Public Administration* 42-2 (Summer 1999), 160-92.

81.<http://www.mmah.gov.on.ca/inthnews/releases/9704031e.htm>

82.For Kingston, see Terrence J. Downey and Robert J. Williams, "Provincial Agendas, Local Responses: The 'Common Sense' Restructuring of Ontario's Municipal Governments," *Canadian Public Administration*, 41-2 (Summer 1998), 226-8; for Grand Bend, see <http://www.mmah.gov.on.ca:80/inthnews/releases/9705091e.htm>.

83.<http://www.mmah.gov.on.ca/inthnews/releases/9707082e.htm>

84. <http://www.mmah.gov.on.ca/inthnews/releases/9704021e.htm>

amendments to labour legislation to allow Pittsburgh employees to enter the Kingston unions with their accumulated seniority rights. The unions were not happy. We do not know, however, what Harris cabinet ministers really thought about their unintended contribution to increased membership in Ontario's public sector unions.

In 1997, the commissioner in Chatham-Kent had stated that "savings of... $12 million for the one-tier option were certainly realistic."[85] In December 1998, the new municipality reported that amalgamation had led to savings of $7 million[86] (total 1995 pre-amalgamation municipal spending was $186 million[87]). By December 1999, the mayor of Chatham-Kent admitted that "the dollar savings are not as great as first thought and that it will be virtually impossible to bring in a budget for 2000 without raising property taxes."[88] The reported annual net savings from amalgamation were by then down to $6.8 million.[89] Of this amount, $890,000 came from merging the operations of the public utilities commissions (PUCs) with those of the municipality.[90] Such a merger did not require amalgamation and must be deducted from the calculated savings. Total one-time transition costs were $19.2 million.[91] Such an amount invested at six per cent annual interest would yield $1.15 million. This then is the opportunity cost of the transition. It must also be deducted from the total, leaving savings from amalgamation at about $4.8 million, or 2.3 per cent of pre-amalgamation operating costs.

In Kingston, the amalgamation agreement among the city and the two townships mandated that total municipal "discretionary expenditures" would be decreased after amalgamation by 15 per cent or $ 7 million, whichever

85. Ontario, *Final Restructuring Proposal*, p.8.
86. Jane Sims, "Tax-fighter watching vision unfold," *The London Free Press*, 21 October 1999.
87. Ontario, Ministry of Municipal Affairs, County of Kent and City of Chatham Restructuring Commission, *Draft Restructuring Proposal for Kent County and the City of Chatham* (1997), p.3.
88. Simon Crouch, "Chatham-Kent mayor warns of tax hike," *The London Free Press*, 31 December 1999.
89. Chatham-Kent, "The Chatham-Kent Experience: A Three-Year Review... 1998-2000 (Draft)" presentation to council, 11 January 2000, p.11. This draft document states the savings at $6.3 million. I have subsequently been informed that the final version will state that the savings are $6.8 million. The discfrepancy arises from pay equity issues.
90. Chatham-Kent, "The Chatham-Kent Experience," p.15.
91. Chatham-Kent, "The Chatham-Kent Experience," p.20.

was the greater amount.[92] In a recent "background information" document about how amalgamations have caused "lower taxes and greater efficiency," the ministry of municipal affairs makes no mention of any savings in Kingston. Had $7 million in savings been achieved, the amount would have ranked only behind the "target" or "anticipated" savings for Toronto and Chatham-Kent, both of which were specifically referred to in the document.[93]

Prior to the 1999 Ontario election, the Harris Conservatives had done nothing to restructure Ontario's two-tier regional governments outside the Municipality of Metropolitan Toronto. Given that the CSR referred to concerns about "regional and municipal levels," this was a surprising omission, unless one assumes that the agenda was being driven more by the traditional concerns of public servants within the ministry of municipal affairs than by the recent concerns of Ontario Conservatives. In any event, despite a lack of any reference to further municipal restructuring in *Blueprint*, its 1999 campaign document, the re-elected government acted quickly in late 1999 to appoint four "special advisors" to make recommendations by the end of November for the restructuring of the two-tier regional-government systems in Ottawa-Carleton, Hamilton-Wentworth, Sudbury, and Haldemand-Norfolk.[94]

The policies of the Harris Conservatives with respect to municipal amalgamations in Ontario can only be properly assessed in the context of the most ambitious amalgamation of all, the one in Toronto, which is the subject of the next chapter.

CONCLUSION

The restructuring of municipal government in New Zealand created two tiers of directly elected local governments. In Australia, such two-tier systems have never existed. In Britain in the 1990s under Prime Minister Major, the object was to eliminate as many two-tier systems as possible by creating new unitary authorities. Now, under Prime Minister Blair, a new upper-tier local authority is being created for Greater London. In Nova Scotia, it appeared that two tiers were to be avoided at all costs, even if it

---

92. Kingston/Frontenac/Lennox and Addington Governance Review Committee, "Proposal for the Reform of Local Governance: Kingston/Frontenac," 10 July 1996, p.28.
93. <http://www.mmah.gov.on.ca/inthenews/backgrnd/1990823-4e.htm>
94. <http://www.gov.on.ca/inthenews/releases/1990823-1e.htm>

meant establishing the gigantic single-tier regional municipalities of Cape Breton and Halifax. In Ontario, two-tier systems were eliminated by amalgamation in Metropolitan Toronto, Chatham-Kent, and in the rural county of Prince Edward. But despite the dozens of restructuring schemes that were implemented, no other two-tier systems were abolished before the election of 1999. After the election, the Harris Conservatives turned their attention to at least some of the two-tier regional systems. Its latest actions are the subject of Chapter 6.

Discerning a pattern in all this is extremely difficult. However, if we eliminate New Zealand as a special case because it is a small unitary state whose central government was intent on substantial decentralization, then we can perhaps at least conclude that recent amalgamations elsewhere have been caused in part by an attempt to avoid or eliminate two-tier systems that were seen as dysfunctional.

But more than this seems to have been going on in Victoria (Australia), Nova Scotia, and Ontario. In these jurisdictions there has been a clear belief within the relevant central governments that municipal politicians and municipalities were inherently wasteful, inefficient, and incapable of co-operating with each other. Notwithstanding evidence to the contrary, the solution was to try to save money and promote economic development by creating bigger municipalities governed by fewer elected councillors. Not all public policy decisions are made on the basis of careful and rational evaluations of alternative courses of action or inaction. Unfortunately, prime examples in the 1990s are policy decisions involving many of the municipal amalgamations discussed in this chapter.

CHAPTER 5

TORONTO'S MEGACITY[1]

In Chapter 2 we looked at the report of the Goldenberg royal commission on Metropolitan Toronto and the subsequent decision of the provincial government led by Premier John Robarts to consolidate Metro's 13 constituent municipalities into six. In the 1970s, after he had left active politics, Mr. Robarts himself was appointed as a one-man royal commission to study Metro yet again. His report, released in 1977,[2] called for a change in municipal boundaries within Metro but no change in the number of constituent units. Such changes were never implemented. The Robarts report also recommended that members of Metro council (other than the six mayors) be directly elected. This recommendation was not acted on until 1988, when the Liberals held provincial office.[3] Also in 1988, the Liberal government established the Office of the Greater Toronto Area (OGTA), a small group of civil servants headed by a deputy minister charged with bringing together the disparate parts of the government whose work affected the wider Toronto area. Its

---

1. This chapter, especially the third, fourth and fifth sections, on the operations of Toronto's megacity, has been prepared with the assistance of Lionel D. Feldman Consulting Ltd. The city of Montreal commissioned its own study of the causes and effects of the megacity. See Don Stevenson and Richard Gilbert, "Restructuring Municipal Government in Greater Toronto," 30 July 1999. The study is available at <http://www.ville.montreal.qc.ca/uneile_uneville/english/une00e.htm> click "related studies."
2. Ontario, *Report of the Royal Commission on Metropolitan Toronto*, (1977), 2 vols.
3. Hugh Mellon, "Reforming the Electoral System of Metropolitan Toronto: Doing Away with Dual Representation," *Canadian Public Administration*, 36-1 (Spring 1993), pp.38-56

territory, known as the GTA, included Metro and the regional municipalities of Halton, Peel, York, and Durham. Its population in 1991 was 4.2 million.[4]

The GTA was badly hit by the recession of the early 1990s. Most of the area's economic problems were far beyond the capacity of municipal government to solve. However, there were serious property tax inequities, difficulties in co-ordinating infrastructure planning, and a widespread belief that different parts of the municipal system were working against each other. In April of 1995, Premier Bob Rae appointed Anne Golden, the president of the United Way of Greater Toronto, to head a five-person GTA task force charged with examining "the region's quality of life, governance, and competitiveness."[5] The work of the Golden task force set off a remarkable series of events, whose outcomes no one could possibly have predicted.

This chapter has five sections. The first describes how the Golden task force dealt with the issue of GTA governance. The second examines the policy-making process on this issue within the Ontario Conservative party, starting from before the 1995 election that brought the party to office and ending with the aftermath of its re-election in 1999. The third, fourth, and fifth sections deal, respectively, with staffing, financial, and governance issues within the new City of Toronto, the "megacity" that came into being on 1 January 1998 as a result of legislation sponsored by the Conservatives in the previous year. Interesting and important as it may be, the protracted battle by Toronto citizens' groups and by opposition parties to prevent the passage of the megacity legislation will not be discussed in any detail;[6] nor will there be any analysis of the unsuccessful legal challenge to the government's megacity legislation.[7]

---

4. Frances Frisken, "The Greater Toronto Area in Transition: The Search for New Planning and Servicing Strategies" in Donald N. Rothblatt and Andrew Sancton, eds., *Metropolitan Governance Revisited: American/Canadian Intergovernmental Perspectives* (Berkeley: Institute of Governmental Studies Press at the University of California, 1998), pp.161-235.
5. Ontario, Task Force on the Future of the Greater Toronto Area, *Greater Toronto: Report of the GTA Task Force* (Toronto: Queen's Printer, 1996), p.9.
6. See Martin Horak, "The Power of Local Identity: C4LD and the Anti-amalgamation Mobilization in Toronto," Research Paper 195, Centre for Urban and Conmmunity Studies at the University of Toronto, November 1998.
7. *East York (Borough) v. Ontario* (1997) 153 D.L.R. (4th) 299 (Ont. C.A.)

THE GOLDEN TASK FORCE[8]

For the purposes of this report, it is the task force's approach to the issue of municipal amalgamation that deserves analysis. There were countless claims by various observers, especially in *The Toronto Star*, that having 30 municipalities in the GTA led to inordinate waste and duplication. Many citizens assumed that municipal amalgamation was a major item on the task force's agenda. For example, the task force received numerous letters from private citizens in East York urging that the borough and its school board not be consolidated with neighbouring areas so that they could continue to provide their own unique mix of local services.[9]

Significantly, there were very few serious proposals made to the task force for radical municipal consolidation. Metro Toronto advocated a new GTA authority comprising the territory of 21 of the 30 existing GTA municipalities. It proposed a modest consolidation, so that there would be 15 new municipalities. Not surprisingly, because of potential political difficulties within Metro council of deciding otherwise, all of the existing Metro municipalities were to remain intact.[10] The city of Mississauga (population 463,000) argued that consolidation should take place in such a way that all GTA municipalities would have populations between 400,000 and 800,000. It claimed that cities with such a population range

> ...can be responsive to the needs of the residential and business community and still achieve excellent municipal management in a business-like manner. The delivery of cross-municipal utility-like services can be handled more efficiently and maximize the potential for public-private partnerships.[11]

8. Much of this discussion comes from Andrew Sancton, "Reducing Costs by Consolidating Municipalities: New Brunswick, Nova Scotia, and Ontario," *Canadian Public Administration*, 39-3 (Fall 1996), 281-3
9. These can be examined in the exceptionally useful CD-ROM that accompanies the Golden Task Force report. It contains not only the printed report and background studies, but also copies of all the written submissions made to the task force.
10.Municipality of Metropolitan Toronto, Chief Administrator's Office, Corporate Planning Division, "There's No Turning Back: A Proposal for Change," August 1995, p.11 (p.1550 in Ontario, *Greater Toronto*, CD-ROM version, Appendix file)
11.City of Mississauga, "Running the GTA Like a Business," August 1995, p.13 (p.1759 in Ontario, *Greater Toronto*, CD-ROM version, Appendix file).

The town of Markham advocated municipal consolidation within York region because "[e]fficiencies of scale remain to be realized." However, it opposed complete consolidation into a single municipality arguing that, "When institutions get too large and cumbersome the supposed economies of scale tend to evaporate and move in the opposite direction... being more costly, less flexible, and less subject to influence by the general public."[12]

Separate briefs from the smaller municipalities of Ajax and Milton argued that smaller municipalities were more efficient than larger ones.[13] Both briefs contained crude quantitative data from Ontario in general and the GTA in particular purporting to show that per capita expenditure increased with size. Crude as the data were, they were at least presented. Consolidationists presented no numbers at all.

The task force's position on consolidation, while noteworthy, received little publicity. It deserves careful attention. The task force pointed out that the cost-saving benefits of consolidation are "often over-stated." Its scepticism was based on two considerations, the first of which was that:

> The cost of delivering services does not always fall as the amount of service increases. In fact, amalgamation can create diseconomies of scale. Moreover, the savings in eliminating administrative duplication can be offset by the upward migration of wages and service standards that often occurs when different wage and service structures are combined.[14]

For this statement the task force cites work by Joseph Kushner and others,[15] as well as the 1992 Price-Waterhouse study prepared for the area municipalities within the Regional Municipality of Ottawa-Carleton. This study claimed that complete consolidation within the area would lead to increased costs because "the efficient, low-cost operational approach of

---

12. Town of Markham, Chief Administrative Officer and Senior Management, "Submission of the Town of Markham to the Golden Task Force," September 1995, pp.2-3 (pp.1470-1 in Ontario, *Greater Toronto*, CD-ROM version, Appendix file).
13. Town of Ajax, "Submission to the Greater Toronto Area Task Force," and Town of Milton, "Bigger is Not Better, Smaller is Smarter: Second Submission to the GTA Task Force," September 1995, pp.4-5 (pp.55-6 and 1737-8 respectively in, Ontario, *Greater Toronto*, CD-ROM version, Appendix file).
14. Ontario, *Greater Toronto*, p.212.
15. Joseph Kushner, Isodore Masse, Thomas Peters, and Lewis Soroka, "The Determinants of Municipal Expenditures in Ontario," *Canadian Tax Journal*, 44-2 (1996), 451-64.

the smaller municipalities would be lost, and would not be compensated for by any significant economies of scale."[16]

The second consideration offered by the task force was this:

> Amalgamation reduces competition between municipalities, potentially leading to less efficiency. With fewer municipalities against which to benchmark, there is less opportunity to measure relative performance and less pressure to keep costs low.[17]

Having made a statement that is quite revolutionary in the Ontario context, the task force then scurried to safer ground:

> Although the Task Force is reluctant to recommend widespread municipal consolidation, we acknowledge that some municipalities, as they are currently configured, will lack the financial capacity to deliver the full range of services the Task Force is proposing. Under these circumstances, we believe consolidation should be pursued.[18]

At this point, the task force wanted to turn the tricky issue over to another institution, in this case its proposed Greater Toronto Implementation Commission. If deciding the appropriate number of municipalities for the GTA is "implementation," it is difficult to know what in this context would have constituted a "policy."

The Golden task force was obviously sceptical about the benefits of large-scale municipal amalgamations. Few people noticed this, however, because its main institutional recommendation involved establishing a relatively powerful, but not directly-elected, Greater Toronto Area Council, which was to act as a new upper-tier authority replacing Metro and the four regional governments. Such a recommendation caused considerable difficulty for the new provincial government led by Premier Mike Harris.

THE HARRIS CONSERVATIVES AND TORONTO'S MEGACITY

In the previous chapter we noted that there was nothing in the *Common Sense Revolution* to suggest that a Harris government would sponsor municipal amalgamations. Judging by the statements of Conservatives in

16. Price Waterhouse, *The Municipalities of Ottawa-Carleton: Study of the Financial Impact of One-Tier Government in Ottawa-Carleton*, 27 August 1992, p.i.
17. Ontario, *Greater Toronto*, p.213.
18. Ontario, *Greater Toronto*, p.213.

opposition, including those of Harris himself, voters might rather have expected a dismantling of the upper-tier regional governments. That a Harris government would be responsible for the largest municipal merger in Canadian history – Toronto's megacity – seemed quite beyond the realm of possibility, even in the months immediately after its election in 1995.

The origins of the megacity decision are difficult to determine. On 5 January 1995, the leader of the then third party in the Ontario legislature appointed the "Mike Harris Task Force Bringing Common Sense to Metro." The chair was Joyce Trimmer, who had retired a few months previous as mayor of Scarborough.[19] She was actively recruited by Mr. Harris to be a Conservative candidate in the approaching election but she adhered to her decision to leave politics. There were three "co-chairs," Al Leach, Derywn Shea, and Morley Kells, each of whom did turn out to be a successful Conservative candidate in June 1995. The task force conducted six public hearings in Metro in February and March 1995, but the members themselves never met alone to discuss their recommendations. According to handwritten notes kept by Ms. Trimmer, none of the approximately 30 presentations recommended a complete merger, although some suggested that there should be four municipalities within Metro rather than six. There were frequent references to the desirability of eliminating Metro, or at least to weakening its authority and reducing its budget.

In retrospect, it appears that the existence of the task force might have had more to do with preparing for the election than with preparing for government. Recruiting Ms. Trimmer would have given the Harris campaign considerable credibility within Metro; she was certainly better known than any of her three co-chairs. Staff support for the task force came from Mr. Harris's office, notably David Lindsay and Tony Clement. At one point David Lindsay sent to Ms. Trimmer "a first cut at an 'Interim Report' from you to Mike." He wrote that he was sending "a copy to Mike in North Bay for his comments and suggestions and I would welcome your thoughts and input."[20] Since Ms. Trimmer was the chair, this last remark seems to speak eloquently as to how people in the leader's office viewed the independence of the task force. The "first cut" that Mr. Lindsay referred to included drafts of a two-page covering letter dated 30 March 1995 and a six-page report. The letter listed eight "findings." None specifically referred to the desirability

---

19. Ontario Progressive Conservative Caucus, "News Release – Mike Harris: Bringing Common sense to Metro Government," 5 January 1995.
20. Handwritten letter from "David" to "Joyce," no date, but accompanying a typed draft of a letter from Joyce Trimmer to Michael Harris dated 30 March 1995.

of eliminating the Metro level of government. However, in a separate paragraph in the letter, the following statement appeared:

[T]hese observations are leading us to conclude that the Metro level of government should be eliminated. Responsibility for the delivery of some services should be moved to the local level; others, such as transportation, should be structured on an expanded regional basis beyond the current Metro boundaries. Some services may have to be assumed by the Province.

The "interim report" was never officially released. Indeed, the four task force members never met to discuss it. There is no evidence that any of them ever signed it. However, on 3 April during a pre-election debate on GTA issues sponsored by *The Toronto Star*, Mike Harris stated that, "Last Thursday, the chair, Joyce Trimmer, presented an update of their work."[21] "Last Thursday" was 30 March, the date of the draft covering letter. During the debate Mr. Harris made a number of specific references to the work of the Trimmer task force. He pointed out that the task force concluded that "there are too many arbitrary political boundaries" and that the task force is leading to the conclusion

...that Metro regional government in its current form must go... Eliminating Metro government would result in the elimination of regional taxation. Under this option, local councils, would negotiate a direct payment for their share of the costs of regional services... This may very well lead to the complete elimination of an entire level of government.[22]

Although it was far from clear in this debate exactly what structural arrangements Mr. Harris did favour, three points were readily apparent: he supported the findings of the Trimmer task force (which, in any event, were drafted in his own office); there was no hint of a megacity; and the Metro level of government was being targeted for elimination.

That the Harris government would end up taking a different position from the NDP-appointed Golden task force is not surprising. That it would go against the findings of its own pre-election party task force, one of whose members became minister of municipal affairs, requires more analysis. There are conflicting journalistic accounts of what happened. William Walker, writing in *The Toronto Star* on 21 December 1996, relied

21.Mike Harris, "Within 180 days of taking office, my government will act," *The Toronto Star*, 4 April 1995, p.A14.
22.Harris, "Within 180 days,"

primarily on an unnamed official within the ministry of municipal affairs. The official claimed that Golden's plan for a GTA council was rejected early on because "we were concerned about creating what would be like a small country, let alone a small province." But if Harris's election promise was to be delivered by abolishing the Metro level of government, the problem then became what to do about Metro-level services. On this issue, Walker quoted David Crombie, former mayor of Toronto, and chair of the "Who Does What" panel that had been appointed by Premier Harris to review provincial-municipal issues throughout the province. Crombie's panel could not reach internal agreement on the Metro issue, but Crombie himself was, according to Walker, adamant that Metro services could not be returned to the municipalities. In fact, Walker claimed that it was Crombie who first seriously proposed the megacity at a meeting in July 1996. Walker quoted his ministry official as saying, "Crombie was the key. When we heard the king of neighbourhoods, the guy who grew up in Swansea, say there won't be damage to neighbourhoods, then we felt pretty good about it intellectually. It just put everybody at ease."

John Ibbitson's account in his book about the Harris government made reference to Crombie only by pointing out that he (like the Golden task force) was more concerned with the GTA as a whole than with municipal structures within Metro.[23] According to Ibbitson, Al Leach was the originator of the megacity. Harris was initially sceptical but was won over by arguments about how amalgamation promoted coherence and global competitiveness while at the same time conveniently eliminating the source of much political opposition: the Toronto city council.[24]

When confronted in the legislature about the apparent conflict between the CSR and the megacity policy, Al Leach stated the following:

> I think by now we've all heard the comment that there was no mention in the *Common Sense Revolution* about amalgamating Metro Toronto. What exactly did we promise in the *Common Sense Revolution*? We said that Ontario would have less government. We said that there should be fewer politicians, there should be less bureaucracy and there should be less overlap and duplication. This legislation will help us reach those goals.[25]

In response to opposition questioning in the legislature, both Messrs. Leach and Harris even claimed that their actions were in accord with the

23. John Ibbitson, *Promised Land: Inside the Mike Harris Revolution* (Toronto, Prentice-Hall, 1997), p.249.
24. Ibbitson, *Promised Land*, p.247.
25. Ontario, *Hansard*, 15 January 1997.

eight major recommendations of the Trimmer report, without mentioning that they contradicted its one central conclusion.[26]

All the evidence seems to suggest that the Harris Conservatives did not come to office favouring municipal amalgamation, either in Toronto or anywhere else. Outside Toronto, it became an issue in late 1995 through Bill 26, the details of which were − it is almost universally acknowledged − driven by a civil service agenda rather than a political one. The aftermath of Bill 26 was discussed in the previous chapter.

Toronto's megacity did not emerge until more than one year after the introduction of Bill 26. The combination of the Golden task force report and Mr. Harris's own election promises about Toronto compelled the government to do something. The Golden recommendations were doomed because they called both for what was clearly a GTA-tier of local government and for inter-municipal service agencies that looked fairly similar to the Metro and regional governments that were supposed to be abolished. The Golden task force never articulated a vision of metropolitan governmental arrangements that would be attractive to anti-government,

---

26. Mr. Leach's remarks were made on 15 January and Mr. Harris's on 21 January. In early January a copy of "The Metro Task Force Summary" began circulating among opponents of the megacity legislation. It bore no date; it was on plain paper with nothing to identify it as having anything to do with the Conservative party or with the Trimmer task force. It is identical to a document within Joyce Trimmer's own files, but the text is not identical to that of the six-page draft report sent to Ms. Trimmer by David Lindsay (see fn.20). Ms. Trimmer explained in an interview with me on 17 November 1998 that she made changes to the first draft and sent a revised copy back to Mr. Harris's office. I now have in my possession three different versions of the Trimmer report, each without a date. They all say essentially the same thing, although the document that circulated in January − and the one that Ms. Trimmer claims is the final draft contains the following statements not contained in the first version:

> ... the task force recommends the elimination of the Metro level of government as the cornerstone of the reform process.

> We must be aware of so-called "false economies of scale" in which smaller operations are subsumed into larger ones for the sake of efficiency but are soon bogged down by the growth of bureaucracy.

It is not clear what version of the Trimmer report the various members of the legislature were referring to, or even if it was the same one. In any event, the eight "major recommendations" referred to by Messrs. Leach and Harris were in the covering letter from Ms. Trimmer, not in the report. It is highly unlikely that the opposition members even knew that this letter existed.

market-oriented Conservatives.[27] The Trimmer party task force attempted such a task, but without any serious intellectual framework and without confronting all the apparent loose ends that would be left from abolishing existing upper-tier governments. Since Harris's public pronouncements at the time of *The Toronto Star* debate focused primarily on eliminating a level of government rather than sketching out alternatives, the government came to office without any clear commitment as to its course of action.

But Harris was committed to "less government." It was not difficult politically to equate "less government" with reducing the number of governments, government agencies, and politicians. Although avowedly free-market promoters such as local chambers of commerce (including the Toronto Board of Trade) often equate the two, no serious analyst would ever make such an obvious mistake. But the position of the chamber of commerce does have a degree of internal logic. Sometimes businesses want a single big government dominated by a few politicians that is capable of resolving big problems over large territories. But such a desire is not the same thing as wanting a single big government because it is cheaper or more efficient. Nobody who has studied the issue seriously has ever arrived at such a conclusion.[28]

When the Harris government started confronting governance issues within the GTA, it discovered that any plan to abolish Metro and the regions actually resulted in a system that, in terms of organizational charts at least, was more complicated. Complexity was seen as the enemy – especially if it involved establishing new inter-municipal boards and commissions to replace metropolitan and regional governments. Such an approach was never a problem for the Thatcher government in Britain, a government that Harris was presumably trying to emulate. But Thatcher clearly understood the difference between less government and fewer governments, between the desirability of reducing the bureaucracy and the desirability of reducing the number of politicians.

Because of its lack of rigorous research and preparation, the Harris government apparently stumbled into the megacity solution. Once the policy was decided, serious debate was not possible. Government spokespersons – from Premier Harris down to officials within the ministry of municipal affairs – could only repeat the mantra: megacity eliminated a

---

27. I tried to make this point in "Assessing the GTA Task Force's proposals on Governance," *Policy Options*, September 1996, pp.38-41.

28. For an important review of the literature and for an innovative approach to this issue, see, see George Boyne, "Population Size and Economies of Scale in Local Government," *Policy and Politics*, 23-3 (1995), 213-22.

layer of government; reduced overlap and duplication; and cut the number of politicians. Such words were congruent with the vocabulary of the CSR. The fact that the policy itself violated its core idea – the need for less government, more efficient government, and more responsive government – was by this stage immaterial. The rest of this chapter is concerned with assessing the experience with the megacity in the period after the legislature approved its creation.

STAFFING ISSUES

As in Halifax, the new amalgamated city council came to office with a CAO and statutory municipal officers already in place. Making these appointments was one of the responsibilities of the Toronto Transition Team, a six-person group (chaired by the Metro chair, Alan Tonks) that was appointed by the provincial government to manage the transition between 25 April and 31 December 1997. The team lacked time and resources and the transition was far from orderly.

Appointing the CAO was one of its more difficult tasks. The team decided that it should appoint no one for a term longer than three years, the length of the council's term. This deterred some candidates who withdrew at the short-list stage. Others withdrew because they accepted other positions during the slow selection process. The man chosen was Michael R. Garrett, a former assistant deputy minister in the Ontario government, who, until his Toronto appointment, was the CAO for the Regional Municipality of Peel. In this capacity he had been a relentless critic of what he and his political masters considered extravagant spending within Metro and its constituent municipalities.[29]

Toronto city council had little choice but to endorse Garrett's appointment in January 1998, even though many councillors considered him lacking in big-city experience. One of Mr. Garrett's initial priorities was to select people to fill other senior executive positions. This was a delicate political operation, requiring a balance from among the former municipalities and care that women and visible minorities were appropriately represented. In the end, all these considerations were accounted for, although former Scarborough administrators came up with nothing in the first round of senior appointments.

---

29. John Lorinc, "Rail to the Chief," *Toronto Life*, April 1999, p.58.

It was decided early on that no outsiders (apart from Mr. Garrett) would be appointed to executive positions. In the early months of the megacity's operation, those who had already been appointed to senior positions (including Mr. Garrett) spent a significant portion of their scarce time interviewing candidates for less senior positions. The candidates themselves were all supposed to be carrying on with their old positions, sometimes under intense pressure to work exceptionally long hours, not having any idea whether or not they would be working for the new city. Morale plunged.

Generous exit options were available. Fortunately, all employees belonged to the same pension plan, the Ontario Municipal Employees Retirement System (OMERS). Under the provisions of this plan, any employee whose age plus years of appointment totalled 80 was eligible to leave at full pension with all benefits. As often happens in these circumstances, many of the most competent staff negotiated an exit package and left immediately rather than face the ongoing uncertainty. Total projected cost by 2000 of the exit packages is $50 million, or 24 per cent of all one-time transition costs.[30] There is a rule that no former executive or management employee who took a voluntary exit package could work in the new city of Toronto for at least two years. There are reports, however, that the rule has been breached, resulting in consulting contracts for former employees worth more than the cost of their former annual salary and benefits.

It is obvious that all has not been well within the senior management team. Part of the problem is that they have been criticized by councillors for not moving fast enough to integrate fully the seven municipal bureaucracies. There have been repeated reports that Mr. Garrett has almost been fired, has almost quit, or that he will leave when his term expires.[31] Meanwhile, of the six "commissioners" reporting directly to the CAO, two have already left, one was dismissed, and the other is now a deputy minister in the Ontario government. On 9 November 1999, the city's deputy mayor was reported as saying that "Toronto is going to have trouble recruiting and keeping senior administrators unless it boosts their pay." Mr. Garrett's salary was reported as being between $185,000 and $190,000;

---

30. City of Toronto, Office of the Chief Administrative Officer, Amalgamation Office, *Building the New City of Toronto: Status Report on Amalgamation*, July 1999, p.71.
31. Lorinc, "Rail to the Chief," pp.57-64.

commissioners about $150,000; and directors (immediately below commissioners) between $100,000 and $145,000.[32]

FINANCIAL IMPLICATIONS

On 23 November 1996 – about three weeks before first announcing his megacity policy – Ontario's minister of municipal affairs, Al Leach, commissioned a study from KPMG, at a cost of $100,000, to assess the financial implications of merging all the constituent parts of the Municipality of Metropolitan Toronto. The results of the study were made public on 16 December.[33] The next day, as part of his announcement, Mr. Leach made the following statement:

> Yesterday, our government released a study prepared by management consultants KPMG.
>
> It showed that over the first three years of its existence, a unified City of Toronto would save $865 million, then $300 million annually from then on.[34]

There are five important points to be made about this statement:

1. Although Mr. Leach acknowledged that "it's not just about money," financial savings were unquestionably the main justification for the policy. Other references to "developing a central core in the GTA and Ontario that is competitive and strong and has international presence in the world market" and to "sweeping away artificial barriers," were not developed. For example, there was no consultants' study – or any other form of juctification – relating to the claim that the global competitive position of Toronto businesses would be improved as a result of amalgamation.

---

32. James Rusk, "Pay too low for top city staff: Ootes," *The Globe and Mail*, 9 November 1999.
33. James Rusk, "Metro to become one big city," *The Globe and Mail*, 17 December 1996, A-1.
34. Partial text of an address by Al Leach to the Toronto Board of Trade, 17 December 1996, reprinted in *The Toronto Star*, 18 December 1996, A-27. A similarly firm statement about projected savings was included in the ministry's press release relating to the KPMG study. See <http://www.mmah.gov.on.ca/inthenews/releases/961216e.htm>.

2. The KPMG study was much more tentative in its conclusions than Mr. Leach suggested. Commenting on the study the day before, Ron Hikel, a KPMG partner, stated: "It's possible that the amalgamation could produce significantly lower savings than we have talked about, or even a negative result, a net increase in expenditures."[35]

3. The study referred to two types of savings: those that would result directly from the amalgamation ($82 to $112 million annually) and those that would result from "efficiency enhancements" ($148 to $252 million annually).[36] There was no necessary connection between amalgamation and the suggested "efficiency enhancements." Indeed some of these enhancements related to services that were already amalgamated – the police service, for example.

4. The study made no reference to the potential for increased costs due to the harmonization of service levels and collective agreements.[37]

5. Mr. Leach made no reference to one-time transition costs, which were estimated by KPMG at between $150 and $220 million.[38]

A month later, at the beginning of the second-reading debate in the legislature on the bill to create the megacity, Mr. Leach was still referring to the KPMG study as an important justification for his action. It should be noted, however, that his language had become more cautious:

> There are literally dozens of studies that have looked at municipal restructuring in the greater Toronto area. That includes a study done by KPMG that showed that amalgamation in Metro Toronto can save taxpayers up to $865 million over the next three years and $300 million thereafter...[39]

---

35. As quoted in Rusk, "Metro to become."
36. KPMG, *Fresh Start: An Estimate of Potential savings and Costs from the Creation of Single Tier Local Government for Toronto*, 16 December 1996, p.2.
37. This was a point made in a document I prepared as a consultant for the city of Toronto. See Andrew Sancton, "Toronto's Response to the KPMG Report," 17 December 1996.
38. KPMG, *Fresh Start*, p.2.
39. Ontario, Legislature, *Hansard*, 14 January 1997 <http://www.ontla.on.ca/hansard/36_parl/session1/house/0197/L144_2.htm>.

As the protracted debate proceeded, government spokespeople tended to make fewer references to the KPMG study. But they kept referring to the elimination of duplication and overlap and the creation of more private-sector jobs. Saving money was supposed to be a result of eliminating duplication and a cause of private sector job creation. By the government's own standards, savings from the megacity were absolutely crucial. This is precisely why so much effort has been expended since 1998 attempting to show that the megacity is indeed saving money. It is also why Mayor Mel Lastman has been so successful in extracting various financial and political concessions from the Harris government.

Mel Lastman, the mayor of North York, campaigned for megacity mayor in late 1997 on the platform that he would not raise taxes. Compared to his main opponent, Mayor Barbara Hall of the city of Toronto, he was clearly an ally of the Harris government. Everything that has happened since 1997 points to at least a tacit understanding between Mel Lastman and the Harris government: Lastman will use his considerable political skills to make the decision to create the megacity look good; in return the provincial government will do everything it can to help Lastman deliver on his pledge not to raise taxes. This does not mean that there is an especially close relationship between the two sides. Indeed, Mayor Lastman has expressed public fury against the government whenever he has thought that it was reneging on its part of the arrangement. It is the fact that the Harris government has generally acted to remove the cause of Lastman's fury that both points to the existence of the understanding and helps explain Mayor Lastman's remarkable popularity. Rarely, if ever, has a provincial government ever been so politically reliant on a mayor of Toronto.

One of the early signs that the provincial government was extremely sensitive to Mayor Lastman's financial requirements was that five days after the megacity formally came into being, the province announced a $50 million grant for the new city and $100 million in interest-free loans to be paid back between 2000 and 2003. A further $100 million loan was to be made available in 1999. In the press release accompanying the announcement, Mr. Leach was quoted as saying:

> The City has committed to reducing costs. We know the new council will make every effort to do that. In fact, previous reports have indicated that restructuring will lead to savings of $240 million [annually]. We also recognize that it will take time to achieve those savings. We are here in the

meantime to provide bridge financing. We are committed to making sure the new City works.[40]

A year after projecting end-state annual savings of $300 million, Mr. Leach had lowered the figure to $240 million.

According to press reports,[41] the financial assistance resulted from an acknowledgment by the government that its recasting of provincial-municipal financial arrangements would have an adverse impact on the new city. Eventually, cost savings from amalgamation were expected to compensate for this but, because the savings were not immediately available, short-term assistance was required. This justification was important for the government so that it could resist claims for financial assistance from other amalgamated municipalities. At the end of April 1998, the megacity council formally approved its first budget, which included as operating revenue the $50 million grant and the $100 million loan. A year later, the city borrowed another $63 million from the province.[42] For both 1998 and 1999, the megacity council was able to approve budgets that did not involve tax increases. Mayor Lastman, with help from the province, kept his promise.

During 1998, megacity residents noticed very few changes in how municipal services were actually delivered. This was because nothing much had changed, except at the management level. City workers simply carried on as before, without being integrated with respect to their day-to-day operations. It was largely because there were so few changes that most residents seemed to believe that amalgamation was a success. Those who had predicted chaos from the megacity were manifestly wrong. In 1999, noticeable change began, but it was gradual and relatively well-managed.

In July 1999, the city of Toronto released *Building the New City of Toronto: Status Report on Amalgamation*. This was an opportunity for Mayor Lastman to demonstrate that he was keeping up his end of the city's arrangement with the province: amalgamation was shown to be saving money. The *Status Report* appeared after the 1999 provincial election campaign (in which amalgamation was not a significant issue) but before the province announced new initiatives aimed at restructuring municipal

---

40. <http://www.mmah.gov.on.ca/inthenews/releases/980105e.htm>
41. *The Globe and Mail*, 4 and 5 January 1998.
42. <http://www.city.toronto.on.ca/ourcity/budgets/operating99/bud_pres/sld008.htm>

government in Ottawa-Carleton, Hamilton-Wentworth, Sudbury and Haldimand-Norfolk.

The formal presentation of the *Status Report* is highly unusual. The opening page is a "Message from Mayor Lastman" addressed to no one in particular. He tells the reader that the report was prepared by "the Office of our Chief Administrative Officer." At the same time that the *Status Report* appeared, the CAO released his own document, *Building the New City of Toronto: CAO's Mid-term Report to the Mayor and Members of Council*. This latter report had the CAO's own name on the cover and was clearly his. The two reports are in no way contradictory, but the fact that one comes from the Office the Chief Administrative Officer and the other from the CAO himself is surely meant to convey some form of distinction. Since they were published simultaneously, it could hardly be an accident.

In any event, the *Status Report* is more substantial and contains at least some financial data. It merits close attention. The main message of the report is that amalgamation has already produced annual savings of $121 million and that by 2000, the figure will be $150 million, an amount the city had targeted in 1998 but which was well below provincial expectations.[43] In 1999, the city's gross expenditures are $5.5 billion. Projected amalgamation savings in 2000 are therefore 2.7 per cent of gross expenditures in 1999. But $4.0 billion is being spent on services that were already amalgamated.[44] Amalgamation savings are compared in the report to the remaining $1.5 billion in expenditures, the amount spent on services that were not previously amalgamated. By this measure, amalgamation savings represent a 10 per cent reduction in expenditures.

The authors of the *Status Report* claimed that the city has surpassed the annual savings projected by KPMG related to consolidation, but has produced no savings from the projected "efficiency enhancements." Here is the explanation.

> [G]iven that the City has a high proportion of unionized staff, these types of internal cost drivers are closely tied to labour agreements. Significant shifts in internal cost drivers are therefore unlikely to occur in the near future.
>
> Council has yet to address the issue of contracting out and outsourcing with respect to a number of municipal services and Council's direction with respect to this issue still has to be determined. It is, therefore, difficult to predict savings arising from this area in the short-run.

---

43. Toronto, *Status Report*, p.10.
44. Toronto, *Status Report*, p.9.

In addition to the above, it should be noted that the Provincial [KPMG] study did not recognize that the seven former municipalities had realized sizeable efficiencies and made reductions in their budgets in the years preceding amalgamation... This had the effect of limiting the potential for further efficiency savings after consolidation.

It is unlikely that the magnitude of efficiency savings estimated in the Provincial study can be readily achieved in the short-run.[45]

Concerning one-time transition costs, we have seen that KPMG had estimated that they would be between $150 million and $220 million. According to the Status Report, the final cumulative amount at the end of 2001 will be $210 million. This amount does not include further net costs, likely more than $100 million, associated with selling surplus civic buildings and consolidating city offices in and around Toronto city hall. One proposal involves building a new city office building immediately north of city hall at a cost of $166 million.[46]

Transition costs of more than $200 million are arguably quite justifiable if the annual return from amalgamation will soon be $150 million. This figure must now be carefully examined. The only table that comes close to meaningfully disaggregating the $150 million is reproduced below. The first thing to note is that we are looking at "City of Toronto Actual Savings in 1998/99" presented in such a way that they are directly comparable to the 1996 KPMG projected savings from consolidation alone (not from "efficiency enhancements"). "Actual Savings in 1998/99" were $134.3 million, not $150 million, because the $150-million figure has yet to be reached. The categories in the table are KPMG categories. They do not relate to the current financial or administrative reporting structures of the new city of Toronto. The first column is KPMG's minimum projected savings from consolidation; the second its maximum; and the third reports the "Actual Savings in 1998/99."

45.Toronto, Status Report, p.18.
46.See The Globe and Mail, 13 November 1999, A-12, and The National Post, 17 November 1999, A-21.

TABLE 4: COMPARISON OF CITY OF TORONTO CONSOLIDATION SAVINGS:
PROVINCIAL (KPMG) ESTIMATES VERSUS ACTUAL SAVINGS ($MILLIONS)

	KPMG MINIMUM	KPMG MAXIMUM	ACTUAL, 1998-99
GENERAL GOVERNMENT	40.0	50.0	27.6
PROTECTION	19.7	31.0	5.8
TRANSPORTATION	3.5	5.4	18.7
ENVIRONMENT	5.0	7.0	20.0
HEALTH	3.0	3.9	7.0
SOCIAL & FAMILY SERVICES	-	-	17.5
RECREATION & CULTURE	8.0	11.0	28.9
PLANNING & DEVELOPMENT	2.5	3.5	8.8
TOTAL	81.7	111.8	134.3

SOURCE: City of Toronto, *Status Report*, p.17.

The first point to note about the table is that for *none* of the categories, including the total, do the actual reported savings fall within KPMG's upper and lower limits. This is in part because the reported actual savings are considerably more than what KPMG projected from consolidation alone. But for two of the eight categories – general government and protection – actual reported consolidation savings were considerably less than what KPMG projected. Since many people assume that the greatest potential for savings is in general government, the Toronto experience is significant. Reducing the number of politicians, CAOs, municipal clerks, treasurers etc. seems not to have been as great a cost saver as had been hoped. The disparities concerning savings from "protection" relate mainly to the fire service, an item that will be analysed later.

Savings in the other categories are indeed impressive. Unfortunately, there is no explanation whatever as to how they have been brought about within each category. There is no mention anywhere in the *Status Report* of any cuts in service (e.g. reduced parks maintenance). It would be surprising indeed if such cuts were not made, because most municipalities are attempting to contain costs by such methods almost as a matter of routine. Savings from any such cuts in the megacity were presumably reported as "actual savings" and compared directly to the KPMG numbers for consolidation savings. There are brief descriptions of reductions in computer systems, office space, yards, fleets, and garages, but no actual dollar amounts are attributed to these reductions, nor are they attributed to the KPMG functional categories. We are told, however, that $4.9 million was saved in insurance costs, a 54 per cent reduction from 1997 costs.[47]

The most mysterious category in the table is that for "social and family services." In the KPMG study, this category consisted of the following items: "General Assistance [welfare], Assistance to the Aged [including homes for senior citizens], Assistance to Children [municipal contribution to children's aid societies], [and] Day Nurseries." The KPMG study rightly noted that, "Because social and family services are organized on Metro-wide lines and are internally integrated, it can be presumed most of the advantages of consolidation have already been achieved."[48] This statement explains why the table above is blank for the first two columns in this category.

The *Status Report* notes that "amalgamation savings are only possible through reductions in expenditures of the amalgamating programs..."[49] How then can the same *Status Report* claim annual amalgamation savings of $17.5 million for services that were already amalgamated prior to 1998? The *Status Report* neither raises this question nor comes close to addressing it. Yet the $17.5 million in reported annual savings in this category amount to more than 10 per cent of the total reported annual savings.

Detective work produces a possible answer. The KPMG report makes no mention of social housing, an item that falls under the jurisdiction of the city's commissioner for "community and neighbourhood services," a title not unlike "social and family services." In its brief discussion of "consolidation activities" within "community and neighbourhood services," the *Status Report* notes that:

> The operations of the two housing companies in the former City of Toronto and Metro Toronto were consolidated into the new Toronto Housing Company, while at the same time implementing Provincial social housing and major operational changes to reduce costs and enhance tenant service.[50]

An amount of $17.5 million annually could not possibly have been saved just by merging the two organizations. Since all kinds of other changes

47. Toronto, *Status Report*, p.28.
48. KPMG, *Fresh Start*, pp.F:1-2.
49. Toronto, *Status Report*, p.10
50. Toronto, *Status Report*, p.68.

were being made concerning provincial-municipal financial arrangements for social housing at the same time, perhaps the reported savings are somehow connected to such changes. It is also possible, of course, that these reported savings have nothing to do with social housing. But if not, where did these reported savings come from?

The 1996 KPMG report did not attach an exact dollar figure to savings from the consolidation of the six fire departments. However, fire costs in 1995 constituted $231 million of $242 million in "protection services" costs that had not already been amalgamated. Since projected savings from the consolidation of "protection services" were in the $20 million to $31 million range, we can assume that at least $15 million of these savings were expected to come from the fire service.[51]

However, according to *The Toronto Star*, the same KPMG had been paid $700,000 in April 1999 to produce for the city a comprehensive report on its fire-service needs. According to the newspaper account of this report, fire-service pre-amalgamation costs in 1997 were $222 million and in 1998, after amalgamation, they were $218 million. But the report recommended the building of six new fire halls (at a cost of $2 million each, not including land) and the closing of two. It also stated that the total number of fire vehicles could be reduced from 133 to 128. In the newspaper article, the fire chief was quoted as saying that 100 new firefighters would be needed to staff adequately the entire city.[52]

In July 1999, city council decided to hire 62 new firefighters in November (to an existing number of 2,691) and 55 more in March of 2000, subject to the fire-service management being able to reduce rates of absenteeism among firefighters. There has been no comprehensive wage settlement for firefighters in the new city of Toronto. Depending on which department they used to work for, some firefighters are making $2,500 less per year than other firefighters performing exactly the same job and working for the same organization.[53] No decisions have yet been made about the fire stations. There will be no savings from amalgamation in the fire service. There will likely be additional costs that would not have been incurred had the amalgamation not taken place.

Now we turn to what is *not* reported in the table. The city expects to spend $210 million on one-time transition costs (excluding net costs of

51. KPMG, *Fresh Start*, B:1-6.
52. Paul Moloney, "Toronto needs six new fire halls: Report," *The Toronto Star*, 9 April 1999.
53. Jennifer Lewington, "City to get 62 firefighters in fall, more if sick days reduced," *The Globe and Mail*, 21 July 1999, A:6.

133

possible new office space). Investing such a sum at an annual interest rate of six per cent would produce $12 million a year. As with Chatham-Kent, if we want accurately to assess the financial benefits of amalgamation, we must therefore deduct the $12 million, because that amount could have been generated merely from investing the transition costs in safe, interest-producing investments.

The *Status Report* has a separate chapter on what it calls "Harmonizing Service Levels and Fees."[54] The chapter describes what has happened with respect to solid-waste collection, winter maintenance, fees for parks and recreation, public health programs, library hours, and boulevard and parking fees – all matters previously under the jurisdiction of Metro's six constituent municipalities. It also notes that harmonization decisions have not yet been made with respect to the following items: residential water service connection repairs; sewer use by-laws; sewer connection blockage inspection and repairs; tree rot removal and grants; downspout disconnections from sanitary sewers; snow management; and water metering. About 87,000 customers, mostly in the old city of Toronto, still have no water meters but as a result of the megacity council's decision on 26 October 1999, $21 million will be spent as a one-time cost to correct this anomaly.[55]

With respect only to the harmonization decisions that have already been made, the *Status Report* concludes that, "The overall result... has been to decrease 1999 net costs by $400,000 but increase annual costs by approximately $9.5 million *annually* once the harmonization decisions are fully implemented over four years."[56] It is, of course, true that on a net basis over the entire city, residents will be receiving $9.5 million in new services and/or reduced user fees. But no one promoted the megacity on the basis that it would lead to *new* expenditures (or user-fee reductions) that people in the various municipalities may or may not have wanted. The *Status Report* clearly and openly reports the $9.5 million in additional costs caused by harmonization, but does not deduct the $9.5 million from amalgamation savings. It should have, because without amalgamation these extra expenses never would have been incurred.

The *Status Report* was written before collective agreements had been signed with any unions representing workers in amalgamated services.[57] It

---

54. pp.29-37. See also, John Lorinc, "Harmonize This," *Toronto Life*, June 1999, pp.55-61.
55. *The Toronto Star*, 27 October 1999, F:3.
56. Toronto, *Status Report*, p.35.
57. Toronto, *Status Report*, p.63.

therefore tells us as much about the financial impacts of amalgamation as mid-season hockey standings tell us about who will win the Stanley Cup. It is true that the contract with the outside workers has since been settled – but all non-wage items, including the harmonization of work practices and fringe benefits, have been sent to mediation and arbitration.

The councillor who knows the most about the city's finances is Tom Jakobek, chair of the council's budget committee. He is a pro-market Conservative "who wants to prove the megacity can work."[58] This is what he said in a television interview on 15 September 1999, after the announcement of an agreement with the city's outside workers:

> I feel like the cleaner at the end of a new year's eve party, and everyone is happy and had a great time, and I am sitting there and cleaning up this mess and wondering what is going to happen. The cost of this... settlement over the next three years could be $100 million or more. The cost of the arbitration portion... could be even larger than that, and the interesting part about that is that's one of the costs of amalgamation. There is a big debate about whether or not the amalgamation of the City of Toronto saved money or didn't save money. Well, I've got to tell you something. If any person who doesn't realize those wages are eventually going to go to the highest, it's a matter of how you do it, is kidding themselves. So the cost of amalgamation is quickly overshadowing the savings from amalgamation, but that is a bigger issue. We will limp through the year 2000 but where we go from 2001 on is anybody's guess.[59]

Harmonization costs for inside workers (of whom there are *three* times as many as outside workers), firefighters, and even for non-union management positions remain outstanding.

In December 1996, Al Leach claimed that after three years Toronto's amalgamation would be saving $300 million annually. A year later he was down to $240 million. A year and a half after that, the city of Toronto was claiming $150 million. Now the evidence suggests that any costs savings from amalgamation are highly unlikely. Two or three years from now it might well be possible to document the net *costs* of amalgamation.

Whatever the final financial verdict on amalgamation, it is obvious that Toronto's medium-term financial situation is not healthy. Its debt rating has recently been downgraded by both major bond rating organizations.

---

58. John Lorinc, "The Making of the Megacity," *Toronto Life*, November 1998, p.123.

59. Transcript of interview with Councillor Tom Jakobek, CBLT (CBC) evening news (6pm), 15 September 1999.

According to one agency, this was because "provincial downloading has significantly increased the extent of the City's financial responsibilities" and because of increased pressure for infrastructure investments.[60] Starting in 2000, there will be no more provincial interest-free loans and existing loans will have to begin to be repaid.[61] Workers will be receiving pay increases. Pressures to spend on new programs will be intense. Unless the province comes to the rescue again, there will be municipal property tax increases. Such considerations seem to have been behind Mayor Lastman's recent ruminations that Toronto would be better off as a province.[62] Such a comment is really about governance, the subject to which we now turn.

GOVERNANCE

With a population of over 2.3 million, the city of Toronto is now more than twice the size of the next populous city, Montreal. The city of Toronto is so big that it takes us into uncharted waters for a Canadian municipality. The council has 58 members. Each councillor is paid $64,000 per year and total annual cost to the city for each councillor is $300,000. There is no executive committee with the legal authority to act alone and there is no party system. Agendas for monthly council meetings – which last for days – have been known to contain 2,000 pages of documents. Despite all this, everyone seems to acknowledge that the council has worked better than anyone could possibly have expected.

Credit is properly given to the leadership of Mayor Lastman. One of his most crucial early decisions was to accept the advice of his closest political supporters and surround himself with a strong personal staff. His office includes five advisors and appropriate clerical support. The advisors are charged with closely monitoring the voting intentions of councillors and of keeping track of each of their personal concerns. Once having decided his own position with respect to issues facing council, Mayor Lastman has

60. Dominion Bond Rating Service, "Bond, Long Term Debt & Preferred Share Ratings: City of Toronto," 16 December 1998. For the downgrade by the Canadian Bond Rating Service, see Bruce Little, "Toronto's debt slides to double-A," *The Globe and Mail*, 18 November 1999.

61. Some councillors suggested in 1998 that the city should simply refuse to repay the loans. Mayor Lastman and Councillor Jakobek expressed the hope that the province would forgive the loans. See Kim Honey, "Loan in hand, council approves budget," *The Globe & Mail*, 1 May 1998.

62. Robert Benzie, "Toronto should be a province: Lastman," *The National Post*, 21 November 1999.

proven remarkably successful in mobilizing different majority coalitions for different issues. Rarely has he lost an important vote.

His skill in garnering positive media coverage is legendary. Once, while senior management was worrying about the latest budget crisis (caused in part by the mayor's insistence that there be no tax increases), Mr. Lastman devoted his attention to trying to prevent the departure of Ginger Spice from the Spice Girls. Media attention lasted for days. He proudly proclaimed to the local media that no mayor of Toronto had likely ever received such international attention. His decision to participate in the Gay Pride parade seemed to capture just the right combination of enthusiastic inclusiveness and sceptical caution. The same could be said of his growing appreciation of the homelessness crisis. Furthermore, every time he defended Toronto's interests against the latest downloading initiative of the provincial government, he received more support, not because he was just another opponent of the Harris government but more because he seemed like a friend of the government who was simply intent on ensuring that Toronto's needs were never forgotten. The fact that he was usually successful in his clashes with the provincial government – for reasons outlined in the previous section – simply added to his popularity. As recently as October 1999, 66 per cent of Torontonians considered that he had done a good job as mayor and deserved to be re-elected.[63]

All this is recounted not because non-Torontonians need to know about Mel Lastman but because, to understand why the megacity seems to have worked so well at a political level, one needs to know why almost every megacity councillor – regardless of ideology or electoral base – is extremely reluctant to cross the mayor. Taking sides against Mel Lastman is dangerous: his staff can see to it that favoured committee assignments never materialize and voters wonder why the mayor's good leadership is being undermined.

The fact that the political success of the megacity is so attributable to the success of the mayor has its own obvious problems. One is that no one knows what will happen when he is no longer there. Will a "strong mayor" system successfully be passed on as part of the megacity political culture by the time Mayor Lastman leaves office, or will his successor be relatively

---

63.James Rusk, "Lastman riding high, Globe poll finds," *The Globe and Mail*, 1 November 1999.

weak because the mayor of an Ontario city has so little legal authority?[64] Another problem – one that was touched on earlier – is that the role of CAO is extremely difficult in Mayor Lastman's environment. Will a strong city administration emerge when everyone knows that the CAO can accomplish virtually nothing – even with his own commissioners – unless he has the mayor's full support?

The city of Toronto is now characterized both by strong political leadership at the centre and by new mechanisms for political decentralization. The city has six community councils, one for each of the former municipalities. Ward boundaries do not cross the old municipal boundaries and each councillor is a member of a community council. East York's has three members; Toronto's (the old city's) has 16. Originally, the idea was to retain and enhance local identity through the community councils. They were given no funds but some purely local decision-making authority, i.e. they were constituted as committees of adjustment so that they could grant minor zoning variances. They debated local zoning changes and received delegations from local citizens but they could not themselves amend by-laws or impose taxes. The general pattern has been that recommendations from community councils are never rejected – or even discussed – by the full council.[65] This has caused some developers to complain that the community councils are too powerful and are likely to reject economically significant projects because of local concerns about parking and traffic.[66]

The role of community councils will have to be clarified. Are they quasi-judicial decision-making bodies? Quasi-judicial advisory bodies? Local sounding boards? Or should they become mini-councils with authority themselves to amend zoning by-laws and allocate modest amounts of money for neighbourhood improvements? What about their boundaries? Should the size of the councils be equalized, thereby eliminating the last remnants of the old municipalities?[67]

---

64. Andrew Sancton, "Mayors as Political Leaders" in Maureen Mancuso, Richard G. Price, and Ronald Wagenberg, eds., *Leaders and Leadership in Canada* (Toronto: Oxford University Press, 1994), pp. 174-89.

65. For a description of an exceptional case, see John Lorinc, "Scarborough Toughs," *Toronto Life*, January 1999, pp.45-9.

66. Paul Moloney, "Councillors too strong in wards, lawyer says," *The Toronto Star*, 3 December 1998.

67. Councillors will soon be forced to address these issues. See the discussion of the *Fewer Municipal Politicians Act* in the next chapter.

Few Torontonians are concerned about such matters. For most, amalgamation has become a non-issue. Poll results are reported in the city's 1999 *Status Report*:

> In the spring of 1999, 70% of Toronto residents stated that they were satisfied with life after amalgamation (Environics Research). Another survey revealed that 66% of Torontonians who stated an opinion felt that amalgamation was a success. (Ekos Research). In June 1999 79% of Toronto residents felt that Council was on the right track in terms of where it was taking the new City of Toronto (Angus Reid Group).[68]

We do not know what would have happened if Mayor Lastman had been unable to keep his promise of no tax increases. Or what would happen if respondents knew (or were told) that, when all the data are available, reported cost savings from amalgamation will likely disappear? Or what will happen in 2001 if taxes go up? Raising these questions is not meant to diminish the truly remarkable political accomplishment that the megacity represents. Less than three years after thousands of citizens were mobilized to fight the megacity's imposition and thousands more voted against it in municipal referendums, most simply accept it as part of life in Toronto. If this is not a political success, it is hard to imagine what could be.

CONCLUSION

The megacity saga began in 1995 when Premier Rae appointed the Golden task force on the Greater Toronto Area. Instead of establishing Golden's Greater Toronto Council, the Harris government opted to merge the six municipalities of Metropolitan Toronto. As all the commentators at the time pointed out,[69] creating the megacity did nothing to bring the larger GTA together or to remedy the financial disparities between Metro and the outer suburbs. In 1998, however, the Harris government did bring in legislation to create the Greater Toronto Services Board (GTSB), which officially came into existence on 1 January 1999 with a minimum of fanfare and publicity. It is the GTSB – functionally weak as it might be – that is the legacy of the Golden task force.

---

68. Toronto, *Status Report,* p.78
69. See, for example, "Mega forum," *The Globe and Mail*, 15 February 1997, pp.D:1-3.

Because its representational system is rightly based on representation-by-population, the new city of Toronto has more than half the votes within on the GTSB. There are, however, procedural safeguards to prevent its complete dominance. It is far too early to judge the effectiveness of the GTSB. However, any assessment of the megacity will eventually have to determine whether its size has helped or hindered regional co-operation throughout the GTA. So far, Toronto councillors have been so preoccupied with their own complex affairs that they have not yet shown much interest in GTA issues.

Between 1988 and 1997, voters in Metro Toronto elected different sets of councillors to two levels of municipal government. Conflict between the two tiers was frequent. Despite this complex two-tier structure (both in Metro and the surrounding regions) there was still no appropriate mechanism for local politicians to address issues that affected the entire GTA. The system was broken. As leader of the third party in the Ontario legislature, Mike Harris in early 1995 set up his own party task force on the issue and promised, if elected, to fix it. After the Harris Conservatives won the 1995 election, they dispensed with their own task force, ignored the findings of the Golden task force relating to municipal amalgamations, and ended up sponsoring the largest municipal amalgamation in Canada's history.

In so doing they unleashed a storm of protest that captured national, and even international, attention. The government faced marches, demonstrations, negative referendum results and a massive legislative filibuster – but it persisted. The legislation passed, a new mayor and council was elected, the megacity came into being on 1 January 1998, and municipal services carried on as before. There were epic battles between the mayor and the provincial government on financial issues and the mayor usually won, thereby increasing both his own popularity and the propensity for most Torontonians to look favourably on the megacity decision.

From the beginning, the government's own measure of success for the megacity was the saving of money and the prevention of municipal tax increases within Toronto. This is precisely why Mayor Lastman has been so successful in wringing financial concessions from the province. As recently as 24 November 1999, Ontario's minister of municipal affairs was stating that "the amalgamation of Toronto has been a success due to the savings that have been achieved."[70] But as this chapter has shown, when all the accounting is complete, it is highly unlikely that there will be any savings at all. Does it therefore follow that the sponsors of megacity will one day acknowledge that their policy failed?

---

70. Jack Lakey, "Trim council, province urges," *The Toronto Star*, 26 November 1999.

CHAPTER 6

MORE CHANGE IN ONTARIO: OTTAWA, HAMILTON, SUDBURY, AND TORONTO (AGAIN)

Municipal restructuring was not a significant issue in the June 1999 Ontario provincial election. In the Conservatives' election platform, *Blueprint*, there was only one reference to the subject. After stating that "We have found plenty of common sense ways to cut government waste and improve efficiency," the following was included as an example: "Reducing the number of municipalities and school boards, resulting in more than 2,200 fewer municipal politicians."[1] There were no other references – nothing about Toronto, about regional governments, or about the desirability of further amalgamations. In fact, Conservative candidates in suburban areas tended to state that there would be no forced amalgamations in their areas. In York region, north of Toronto, the provincial minister of transport promised his electors that a re-elected Conservative government would not impose amalgamations in the suburban (905) Toronto area.[2] The most outspoken Conservative candidate on this issue was Toni Skarica, an MPP seeking re-election in suburban Hamilton-Wentworth. He told his electors that he had received assurances from the premier's office that there would be no imposed amalgamation in the Hamilton area. He promised that as long as he was their MPP, the Conservatives would not implement such a scheme.[3]

---

1. Progressive Conservative Party of Ontario, *Blueprint*, 1999.
2. Gail Swainson, "Tories won't impose amalgamation: Palladini," *Toronto Star*, 20 May 1999.
3. John Ibbitson, "Drastic promises require drastic measures," *The Globe and Mail*, 30 November 1999. Mr. Ibbitson quotes Paul Rhodes "speaking on behalf of Mr. Harris" during the campaign as follows: "'It is not the party's position to impose a solution... Our position on restructuring in the Hamilton-Wentworth region is that it should be a local solution, and we're looking to local options and local solutions to be brought forward.'"

Less than three months after the election, the new minister of municipal affairs announced that he was taking action "to protect taxpayers in the Regional Municipalities of Haldimand-Norfolk, Hamilton-Wentworth, Ottawa-Carleton and Sudbury from the costs of large bureaucracy, increased red tape and inefficient municipal government."[4] Within four months after that, the Ontario legislature had established new single-tier amalgamated municipalities to take effect on 1 January 2001 in Hamilton, Ottawa, and Sudbury. In the more rural area of Haldimand-Norfolk, the two-tier regional government was dismantled and replaced by two new single-tier municipalities, Haldimand and Norfolk All this was accomplished by a single new law, the *Fewer Municipal Politicians Act, 1999*, which also reduced the size of the Toronto city council from 58 members to 45. This chapter analyses what has happened in Hamilton, Ottawa, Sudbury, and Toronto. Haldimand-Norfolk is less relevant to the central concerns of this report and will be discussed only to the extent that it demonstrates what can happen to regional services when a regional government is abolished.

RESTRUCTURING CONTROVERSIES PRIOR TO 1999

Two-tier systems of regional government were established for Ottawa-Carleton in 1969, Sudbury in 1973, and Hamilton-Wentworth in 1974. From the very beginning they were controversial and unpopular, seen by many as the cause of growing municipal bureaucracies and higher property taxes. Formal reviews of the various systems began soon after they were established. As early as 1978, a three-member panel examining Hamilton-Wentworth concluded that a new single-tier "City of Wentworth" should replace the region and its six constituent municipalities.[5] Ottawa, and to a lesser extent Sudbury, were also examined on a regular basis, but it took much longer in these places for the single-tier solution to emerge as a serious alternative.

All three systems were originally modelled on the post-1966 Municipality of Metropolitan Toronto, except that Ottawa-Carleton, even as late as 1999, comprised 11 separate municipalities, including the village of Rockcliffe Park with a population of only 2000. Ottawa-Carleton's regional

---

4. Ontario, Ministry of Municipal Affairs and Housing, "Gilchrist acts to protect tax-payers: Fewer municipal politicians, improved local government," 23 August 1999 <http://mmahgov.on.ca/inthenews/releases/1990823-1e.htm>

5. Ontario, *Report of the Hamilton-Wentworth Review Commission* (Toronto: 1978).

police force was not created until 1994. Regional councils were originally composed of mayors and councillors from the lower-tier municipalities. Functional responsibilities included police, social services, major roads, and water supply and sewage systems. Costs were apportioned to each municipality in proportion to its share of assessed value of all the real property in the region.

The Hamilton-Wentworth system was dysfunctional almost from the very beginning. The main problem was that the city of Hamilton, because of its high proportion of the regional population (322,000 of 468,000 in 1996), always held more than half the seats on regional council. In the early years of Hamilton-Wentworth, suburban members would sometimes thwart the city by walking out, thereby preventing a quorum. But the more general criticism was that even though regional councils were responsible for some very important decisions, few citizens were much aware of what they were doing. For example, regional issues were rarely a subject of concern in local elections, notwithstanding the fact that many winners automatically ended up on regional council.

The answer to this perceived problem was to provide for some form of direct election to regional council. Direct election of the regional chair was eventually implemented in all three regions. But Ottawa-Carleton, starting in 1994, experienced the most complete form of two-tier municipal government ever known in Ontario. As of that year all regional councillors were directly elected to serve only at that level; some of their wards crossed municipal boundaries; and local mayors were excluded from the regional council. Such changes certainly provided for a more direct method of formal electoral accountability, and they raised the visibility of regional issues. They also, not surprisingly, heightened the impression among local residents that they were over-governed and that the two distinct levels of municipal government were constantly squabbling.

While the Harris government eliminated the two-tier system in Metropolitan Toronto, it did nothing to restructure the other two-tier regional governments. Since at least 1996, all of them have experienced bitter battles between the two tiers, as each side jockeyed for position in the restructuring sweepstakes. Nowhere were the battles more bitter than in Ottawa and Hamilton. A full account of all the manoeuvres in these cities would take up many pages, leaving the reader wondering how such travesties could ever have been allowed to develop. The only beneficiaries were the consultants, facilitators, and mediators, none of whom in the end accomplished anything.

The phrase "the status quo is not an option" has become a great cliché of our time. It is certainly a favourite of ministers in Ontario's Harris government. With respect to regional governments in Ontario, the cliché happens to be true. Although two-tier regional government has its inherent problems, it is not completely unworkable. What *is* unworkable is a system in which each tier has equal political status and in which each is at risk of being abolished. In such circumstances, even the most innocuous everyday issues mutate into nasty political disputes about who should be doing what. Ottawa and Hamilton in recent years provide more examples of this than one would ever want to document.

THE SPECIAL ADVISORS

On 23 August 1999, Steve Gilchrist, the new post-election minister of municipal affairs, promised that he would take action. He said that within 30 days, he would appoint a "special advisor" for each of the four priority areas. Within 60 days after that, each special advisor was to submit a report, after which "Cabinet will act."[6]

Mr. Gilchrist had been parliamentary assistant to Al Leach and had proven himself during Toronto's megacity debate to be one of the few Conservative MPPs capable of defending the government's position. His appointment as minister was a sure sign that notwithstanding *Blueprint* and the election campaign, municipal restructuring would be back on the government's agenda. Unfortunately for Mr. Gilchrist, he only lasted as minister for a few months.[7] Mr. Gilchrist's replacement, Tony Clement, retains his position as minister of the environment, a burden that would have been exceptionally heavy even if Mr. Gilchrist's significant municipal restructuring had not already been launched.

On 24 September, Mr. Gilchrist appointed his special advisors: Glen Shortliffe, former clerk of the privy council for Ottawa-Carleton; David O'Brien, the city manager of Mississauga for Hamilton-Wentworth; Hugh Thomas, retired city manager of Chatham-Kent for Sudbury; and Milt Farrow, a retired senior provincial public servant for Haldimand-Norfolk. In assessing options for municipal structures in their respective areas, the

---

6. Ontario, "Gilchrist acts,"
7. Mr. Gilchrist has not been re-appointed to the cabinet.

special advisors were asked to consider how best to achieve the following objectives (emphasis in original):

Fewer municipal politicians while maintaining accessible, effective, accountable representation, taking into consideration population and community identity.

Lower taxes by reducing overall municipal spending, delivering high quality services at the lowest possible cost, preserving voluntarism, and promoting job creation, investment and economic growth.

Better, more efficient service delivery while maintaining taxpayer accessibility.

Less bureaucracy by simplifying and streamlining government, reducing duplication and overlap, and reducing barriers and red tape for business.

Clear lines of responsibility and better accountability at the local level by reducing duplication and overlap.[8]

In relation to objectives of municipal restructuring advanced in other parts of the world at other times, the fact that "fewer municipal politicians" was placed first on the list seems unusual, but it is totally consistent with the rhetoric of the Harris government's first term and with its proud statement of accomplishment in the *Blueprint* document. Notable because of their absence, were any references to city-suburban equity, controlling the outward expansion of the city, and economic development.

Each of the special advisors held public hearings. Arguments for and against amalgamation were trotted out one more time. In Ottawa, Hamilton, and Sudbury, suburban opposition focused on avoiding a single-city solution. To that end, some suburbs accepted the need for some amalgamations, presumably to show that they were sensitive to the government's objectives. In adopting this strategy they faced two main difficulties. First, it was difficult to argue (as they did) that the creation of three or four new amalgamated municipalities in a city-region would save money, but that the creation of one municipality would not. Second, they had great trouble developing a plan whereby regional services (police, water and sewer, social services) would continue to be delivered by some form of regional authority even after regional government had been abolished.

8. Ontario, Ministry of Municipal Affairs and Housing, "Terms of Reference for Special Advisors," <http://www.mmah.goc.on.ca/inthenews/backgrnd/19990924-2e.asp>

In Ottawa, Hamilton, and Sudbury, the special advisors rejected all such suburban arguments. In the rural area of Haldimand-Norfolk, Mr. Farrow did recommend abolishing the regional government. It is therefore important to know how he dealt with the issue of regional services. For police, he recommended that there be a joint police services board for the two municipalities and that costs be assessed to each on the basis of its share of the assessment. He did not specify what would happen if the two new municipal councils had differing views as to the acceptability of an annual budget adopted by the police services board. Most other regional services would be provided by Norfolk under contract to Haldimand, with the latter paying on the basis of its share of the total assessed value of property in the two municipalities. Some services, however, would be paid for on the basis of usage. For example, Norfolk would continue to use landfill sites located in Haldimand. Other regional functions – such as homes for the aged – were simply assigned to both municipalities because each had appropriate facilities within its borders.[9] Interesting as Mr. Farrow's recommendations were, it is obvious that it would have been significantly more difficult to apply them if more than two new municipalities had been involved.

The three other special advisors rejected the notion that regional governments could be replaced by anything other than an amalgamated municipality. The most forceful rejection came from Mr. Shortliffe: "The establishment of a management/service authority to deliver services currently provided by the RMOC [Regional Municipality of Ottawa-Carleton] is simply replacing the existing two-tier system with another, and runs the risk of being managed by bureaucrats."[10]   He went on to quote with approval an unpublished paper by Harry Kitchen, a Canadian expert on municipal finance, who argues that, "Regardless of what service boards are called and how they are structured, it [sic] is a two-tier system of municipal government and more importantly , a two-tier system that is inferior to the current structure."[11] Both Mr. Shortliffe and Professor Kitchen were equally dismissive of inter-municipal agreements, the solution generally favoured by Mr. Farrow for Haldimand and Norfolk.

---

9. Ontario, Ministry of Municipal Affairs and Housing, "Report of the Special Advisor, Haldimand-Norfolk Review, Milt Farrow," November 1999, pp.19-20.
10. Ontario, Ministry of Municipal Affairs and Housing, "Report to the Minister: Local Government Reform in the Regional Municipality of Ottawa-Carleton," 25 November 1999, p.25.
11. As quoted in Ontario, "Ottawa-Carleton," 25 November 1999, p.30.

There were two other common features of the three reports favouring complete amalgamation. They all favoured a form of "area rating" whereby different tax rates would be levied in different parts of the new amalgamated city depending on which services were actually available. More significantly in light of subsequent developments, they all rejected the notion that tax rates of property owners should be adjusted to take account of the assets and liabilities of the former municipalities in which their properties were located. This was an especially sensitive issue in Ottawa-Carleton where the city of Ottawa had a high debt load and the city of Nepean had substantial capital reserves. Each of the three independent special advisors quoted the same 1953 decision from the Ontario Municipal Board (OMB), which seemed to imply that the amalgamation of municipalities should not result in any form of "individual or collective compensation" relating to the assets and liabilities of the prior municipalities. However, as Hugh Thomas makes clear in his report on Sudbury, the OMB ruling related explicitly to physical assets (city halls, libraries, parks, roads, etc.) and seemed to be silent with respect to financial assets. In any event, Mr. Thomas's position with respect to compensation for financial assets was identical to that of his two colleagues: they all agreed that financial assets and liabilities should simply be pooled in the new city, and none made reference to any form of compensation.[12]

Although Messrs. Shortliffe, O'Brien, and Thomas each recommended complete amalgamation, they inevitably arrived at this conclusion in slightly

---

12.For Thomas, see attachment to letter from Hugh Thomas to Tony Clement dated 25 November 1999, item 22; for Shortliffe, see Ontario, "Ottawa-Carleton," pp.6-1; for O'Brien, see Ontario, Ministry of Municipal Affairs and Housing, "Report to the Minister of Municipal Affairs and Housing: Local Government Reform for Hamilton-Wentworth," 26 November 1999, pp.56-8. Interestingly, two of the independent special advisors used exactly the same language on this issue. The following text appears word-for-word in each document (p.60 and p.57 respectively), with no attribution to another source (sentences before and after in both documents are very similar to each other, but not identical) :

> Proponents of the charge back would suggest that the surpluses were created through the tax rate paid by ratepayers of ["in" is used by O'Brien] the former municipalities. The counter argument is that the state of the infrastructure of each municipality must be assessed before any charge back is considered as any repairs in the future will then be funded through the tax rate of the new municipality.

The 1999 paper by Harry Kitchen ("Ontario: Municipal Funding Responsibilities") that is referred to approvingly by both Thomas and Shortliffe, supports Thomas' interpretation of the meaning of the 1953 OMB decision (p.21.)

different ways. Each will now be examined in turn. In Ottawa-Carleton, Mr. Shortliffe was dealing with 11 lower-tier municipalities having a total population in 1996 of 721,000. Four of the municipalities – with a combined population of 64,000 – were primarily rural in character, even though they each contained many urban settlements comprising people who commuted elsewhere in the region to work. The four municipalities had previously formed a "Rural Alliance," committed to enabling each of its members to separate from the region while establishing a common "Service Management Board" to purchase services for its members from other municipalities or from its own member municipalities.

This is what Mr. Shortliffe had to say about the Rural Alliance:

> The debate in Ottawa-Carleton on the issue of "rurals in" or "rurals out" is an important and sensitive issue, particularly from the perspective of the four rural municipalities. Frankly, no issue debated in the region gave me greater concern. Fear that a "way of life" was threatened was real. There are significant differences between the rural and urban municipalities. Different issues are at play.[13]

He then went on to list the "compelling reasons to recommend the inclusion of the rural municipalities in my proposed model." These involved the close economic links between the urban core and the rural areas; the fact that nine villages in the rural municipalities receive water from the regional system; and the need for comprehensive planning for the entire urban and rural ecosystem. He was also concerned that a new urban municipality would not agree to provide social services to the rural areas on a "case load" basis. Such an arrangement would effectively have reduced the rural share of the region's social service costs because its share of the region's welfare recipients was disproportionately low.

Mr. Shortliffe's conclusion was that:

> The Rural Alliance concept is also based on the premise that the rural municipalities will provide/purchase all required services. However, in my opinion, the rural municipalities have an insufficient tax base to maintain these services without subsidies. As a result, rural municipalities will be required either to increase taxes or attract more development, which in turn will heighten the potential for urban-like sprawl...

> The Rural Alliance in my judgement is not a viable option.[14]

---

13. Ontario, "Ottawa-Carleton," 1999, p.27.
14. Ontario, "Ottawa-Carleton," 1999, p.28.

Mr. Shortliffe recommended that the new amalgamated city have a directly elected mayor and one councillor from each of the 18 wards. Although he included a map of the wards, he did not state their populations. This makes it impossible to know how closely he adhered to the principle of representation-by-population. In any event, he recommended that at least for the first two terms of the new council, the two councillors from the four former rural municipalities (and the rural area of a fifth) be given two votes each.[15] These two councillors would represent about 80,000 – or 11 per cent – of the new city's 721,000 people (1996 figures), but they would control four – or 19 per cent – of council's 21 votes. By favouring the rural areas in this way, Mr. Shortliffe was clearly undermining the principle of representation-by-population and diluting the voting strength of centre-city residents.

Mr. Shortliffe also addressed the desirability of creating community councils or committees within the new cities. His conclusion was that in order to be effective, they must have decision-making authority, but if they were given such authority, a two-tier system would have been re-established, an alternative that was unacceptable.[16] Mr. Shortliffe's solution was, "subject to the city's operating policies," to make individual ward councillors responsible within their respective wards for such matters as parks, recreation, community services, cultural events, libraries, ice rink rentals and time allocations, sidewalk and road maintenance, garbage collection, animal control, temporary road closures, and appointments to community centre boards[17]. He calls such arrangements "wardism." He claims that, "In Canada, very few cities have successfully implemented such political structures."[18] In fact, none have.

Other recommendations involved creating an administrative structure with a CAO (chief administrative officer) and *six* deputy CAOs, each of whose salary would be in the $125,000-$145,000 range.[19] He wanted the new city to have neither a library board nor a police services board,[20] changes which would require amendments to provincial legislation covering the entire province. His most publicized recommendation was "that the

---

15. Ontario, "Ottawa-Carleton," 1999, p.41.
16. Ontario, "Ottawa-Carleton," 1999, p.29.
17. Ontario, "Ottawa-Carleton," 1999, p.45.
18. Ontario, "Ottawa-Carleton," 1999, p.29.
19. Ontario, "Ottawa-Carleton," 1999, p.43.
20. Ontario, "Ottawa-Carleton," 1999, p.47.

enabling legislation establish and designate the City of Ottawa as officially bilingual in English and French."[21]

The Shortliffe plan involved reducing the number of elected municipal officials from 84 to 19. On the cost-savings front, his financial advisors (two firms of chartered accountants) told him that amalgamation itself would save $56 million annually. They assumed, however, that the level of service would remain "as is" and that there would be "an average levelling of salaries." An additional $14-$27 million "is available from annual efficiency gains in program spending."[22] Curiously, there was no reference in the report to existing levels of spending, so the reader is given no idea as to the meaning of the projected savings figures. In 1997, total municipal spending in Ottawa-Carleton was $1.439 billion. Projected amalgamation savings ($56 million) are 3.9 per cent of this figure. But the municipalities that are being amalgamated spent only $453 million in 1997.[23] In relation to this figure, projected amalgamation savings are 12.4 per cent, higher than the 10 per cent claimed by the new city of Toronto. Despite the obvious optimism of the projections, Mr. Shortliffe recommended that "the enabling legislation establish, as a requirement in law, that the City of Ottawa achieve annual savings of $75 million by December 2003."[24] He made no recommendation as to what should happen if the new city council failed to implement such a legal requirement.

One-time transition costs were estimated at $51 million,[25] or 11.5 per cent of the total annual spending of the municipalities being amalgamated. In 1999, the new city of Toronto reported that its equivalent figure was 14 per cent. Mr. Shortliffe's financial advisors were in effect claiming that the Ottawa-Carleton amalgamation would save relatively more money than Toronto's did and that the transition costs would be relatively less.

In Hamilton-Wentworth, special advisor David O'Brien faced a two-tier system comprising six lower-tier municipalities with a total population in 1996 of 468,000. Compared to Mr. Shortliffe, he seemed to have less difficulty arriving at the conclusion that all municipalities should be merged into one. Like Mr. Shortliffe, he recommended a form of special treatment for rural areas. Under his plan for a directly elected mayor and 13

---

21. Ontario, "Ottawa-Carleton," 1999, p.38.
22. Ontario, "Ottawa-Carleton," 1999, p.56.
23. KPMG Ottawa, "Project Report: Ottawa-Carleton Restructuring Options – A Financial Analysis," prepared for the regional Municipality of Ottawa-Carleton, 25 August 1999, Appendix B.
24. Ontario, "Ottawa-Carleton," 1999, p.68.
25. Ontario, "Ottawa-Carleton," 1999, p.66.

councillors from 13 wards, he recommended that the four wards in the former municipalities of Glanbrook, Flamborough, Ancaster, and Dundas have an average population of 28,354, while the nine wards entirely within the former cities of Hamilton and Stoney Creek have an average population of 39,144.[26] Unlike Mr. Shortliffe, Mr. O'Brien did not suggest that individual councillors have any special authority to allocate funds or make decisions relating to facilities within their wards. Like, Mr. Shortliffe, he rejected suggestions that community councils be established.[27]

A peculiar feature of Mr. O'Brien's report is his claim that the two suburban cities (with populations of 80,000 and 65,000, respectively) proposed by the existing five suburban municipalities would not have "enough economic strength to survive, given the fact that more than 90 % of the commercial and industrial assessment [within the region] is within the [existing] City of Hamilton."[28] Here the reader is being told that it is the suburban area that is too weak financially. If the upper-tier regional government is to be abolished, suburban municipalities, even if they are amalgamated, cannot survive financially on their own. Perhaps this is true for the Hamilton area, but it is clearly a dramatically different kind of argument from that advanced in Montreal.

A related point is Mr. O'Brien's claim that, "Most importantly, the economics of survival as an urban entity almost by itself dictates that the area must join as one to be able to compete in the world marketplace."[29] This remarkable statement seems to imply that if the allegedly financially-weak suburbs are not attached to the central city, then such major employers as Stelco, located within the central city, will not be able to sell steel competitively. Such a notion is too absurd to be taken seriously.

Concerning projected financial savings, Mr. O'Brien faced a quite different environment in Hamilton-Wentworth compared to Ottawa-Carleton and Sudbury. This was because the regional government and the city of Hamilton had *already* merged their administrative operations. The city and the region even share the same city manager. Here is how Mr. O'Brien described the situation:

> The administrative structures of the region of Hamilton-Wentworth and the City of Hamilton were combined in 1998 with a saving of approximately $13.6 million in the first year. A further $5.9 million in savings is expected in

26. Calculated from figures in Ontario, "Hamilton-Wentworth," 1999, p.41.
27. Ontario, "Hamilton-Wentworth," 1999, p.43.
28. Ontario, "Hamilton-Wentworth," 1999, p.37.
29. Ontario, "Hamilton-Wentworth," 1999, p.37.

> 1999. Unfortunately, the Regional Council and the City Council remain as separate political entities. This consolidation means that 91% of the total expenditure of local governments in this area is already centred within one administration.[30]

Because of this administrative consolidation, Hamilton-Wentworth was clearly the most innovative regional government in Ontario. It had accomplished what many thought impossible: the establishment of a single administrative apparatus reporting to two different political masters. Tragically, this experiment has never been properly evaluated. Apparently no one defended it in Mr. O'Brien's public hearings because he reports that "there was little or no support for the status quo, and in particular no support at all for the Regional level of government."[31]

Mr. O'Brien was able to find only $10 million in additional savings resulting from amalgamation.[32] In 1998, total municipal operating expenditures in the region were $870 million, which means that the projected savings are 1.1 per cent. Operating spending of lower-tier municipalities was $258 million.[33] On the basis of this number, projected savings are 3.9 per cent. Perhaps because these numbers are so modest, Mr. O'Brien goes further than the other special advisors in recommending that the provincial government take action so as to enable the new council to control costs. He urges that the Provincial government legislate "average levelling" for wage adjustments and that it legislate $10 million in annual savings.[34]

To help city council accomplish these objectives, Mr. O'Brien devoted more attention to "labour issues" than the other special advisors did. He began with these words:

> Issues relating to labour have traditionally been the most difficult for newly restructured municipalities. This, clearly, has been the case in the creation of the new Cities of Toronto and Kingston. It is in everyone's best interests that a climate of labour stability be created by balancing rights and perspectives on workplace issues.[35]

---

30. Ontario, "Hamilton-Wentworth," 1999, pp.28-9.
31. Ontario, "Hamilton-Wentworth," 1999, p.31.
32. Ontario, "Hamilton-Wentworth," 1999, p.55.
33. Ontario, "Hamilton-Wentworth," 1999, p.20.
34. Ontario, "Hamilton-Wentworth," 1999, pp.61 and 54.
35. Ontario, "Hamilton-Wentworth," 1999, p.58.

He recommended that various exceptions in Ontario's labour law be legislated for Hamilton-Wentworth, including one that would be sure to infuriate the affected unions: "That all 'contracting out' provisions of existing agreements be suspended until a new contract can be negotiated."[36]

Mr. O'Brien projected total one-time transition costs to be $10 million.[37] Perhaps, however, from the government's point of view, the most important figures in his report were those relating to the recommended reduction in the total number of elected municipal politicians, from 59 to 14.

The Sudbury report is the least ambitious of the three. Mr. Thomas dealt with an area comprising seven lower-tier municipalities with a total population of 162,000. Unlike the other special advisors, he recommended that the new amalgamated city have a territory slightly larger than that of the existing regional municipality. He recommended that a municipally unorganized area with a population of slightly over 1,000 be added to the new city.[38] Mr. Thomas noted that 30 per cent of the area's population have French as a mother tongue and that French is the predominant language in the municipality of Rayside-Balfour.[39] Nevertheless, unlike Mr. Shortliffe, he decided to leave language policy issues to the transition board and the new council, recommending only, "That in the communities where French is the predominant language, the front line staff provide services in both official languages."[40]

Financial data in Mr. Thomas's report were limited. He stated that two firms of chartered accountants

> ...have reviewed both the estimated savings and transition costs. They have concluded that a savings of $8.5 million [in annual operating costs] is realistic and achievable with a single-tier governance... Financial advisors have reviewed the submissions and estimate the one-time transitional costs to be $12 million.[41]

The text of his report contains no information about total annual operational spending by municipalities in the Sudbury region. The report is much more clear, however, about the recommended reduction in the total number of elected municipal politicians: from 68 to 13.[42]

---

36. Ontario, "Hamilton-Wentworth," 1999, p.61.
37. Ontario, "Hamilton-Wentworth," 1999, p.52.
38. Attachment to letter from Hugh Thomas, item 11.
39. Attachment to letter from Hugh Thomas, item 6.
40. Attachment to letter from Hugh Thomas, item 23.
41. Attachment to letter from Hugh Thomas, item 25
42. Attachment to letter from Hugh Thomas, Table 5.

All the reports show many signs of being hurried. Ironically, for each of the four regions studied, there are a number of much longer, more comprehensive, more thoughtful, better researched, and better written reports that have been written over the past two or three decades. Most of *their* recommendations were never implemented. In the case of these four reports, however, legislation was introduced within days. The legislation called for amalgamation in Ottawa, Hamilton, and Sudbury and dismantling of the regional government in Haldimand-Norfolk. Contrary to most media reports, the proposed legislation generally did not implement most of the other recommendations contained in the special advisors' reports. The government's decision to ignore Mr. Shortliffe's recommendation about official bilingualism for Ottawa was the rule rather than the exception. The legislation dealt with other issues as well, including the size of Toronto's city council.

THE FEWER MUNICIPAL POLITICIANS ACT, 1999

Until a few days before the legislation was introduced, no one knew that the size of Toronto's city council was a current concern of the Harris government. The position of the former minister of municipal affairs, Steve Gilchrist, was that it was up to the Toronto city council to decide whether or not to reduce its membership. Under the new minister, Tony Clement, the position changed. In late November 1999, not long after Mayor Lastman publicly wondered about the desirability of Toronto leaving Ontario, Mr. Clement wrote to the mayor and informed him that the government would soon be introducing new local government legislation. He continued:

> This reform initiative provides us with an opportunity to enter into a dialogue with the city of Toronto.
>
> In particular, some members of your council and the public suggest that a 58-member council is large, costly and unwieldy. Therefore, I ask what measures your council would propose to reduce the number of politicians and achieve tax savings.[43]

---

43. As quoted in James Rusk, "Size of council just fine, Lastman says," *The Globe and Mail* 26 November 1999.

Mayor Lastman rejected the need for a reduction in the size of the council and replied to Mr. Clement by stating that, "Our council is efficient and representative of our city and our city's diversity."[44]

Subsequent newspaper reports suggested that some right-wing Toronto city councillors, especially Tom Jakobek, had convinced a Toronto cabinet minister, Chris Stockwell, that action needed to be taken. Since Premier Harris had good reason to be annoyed with Mayor Lastman, he supported Mr. Stockwell's position. On 2 December 1999 Mr. Clement announced at a press conference that Toronto city council had less than three days to decide whether their number was to be cut to 44 or to 22. In either case, the basis of the new wards would be the 22 federal electoral districts within the city, the same ones that had already been adopted for provincial purposes as well.[45] During the three-day period, city council did not meet, but it was obvious that most councillors preferred that the number be 44 rather than 22.

Mr. Clement knew, of course, that 44 would be the choice. At his press conference he released a brief statement outlining "the case for fewer politicians in the City of Toronto." The statement claimed that the original size of the council was "a transitional measure" and that since 1998 "despite the clear benefit for taxpayers of a smaller council, Toronto has not exercised its power to bring council to a manageable level." Figures were presented showing that with 56 councillors and a mayor, citizens of Toronto had a lower citizen-to-councillor ratio than each of the following North American cities: Calgary, Edmonton, Vancouver, Chicago, New York, Los Angeles, Houston, Dallas, and Mississauga. Since each Toronto councillor costs the municipality $300,000 a year, the reduction was expected to save $4 million a year.[46] The release did not make reference to one obvious corollary of the government's decision: since the new electoral districts would cross the boundaries of the old municipalities, it would be impossible to maintain community committees with the same boundaries as the old municipalities.

On 6 December, Mr. Clement introduced into the legislature the *Fewer Municipal Politicians Act, 1999*. This one, omnibus bill reduced the size of the Toronto city council from 58 to 45, established new systems of

---

44. As quoted in Rusk, "Size of council."
45. Richard Mackie, "Ontario bill would slash Toronto city council by 13," 1 December 1999 and Michael Valpy, "City council a victim of Harris, Lastman testosterone battle," 4 December 1999, *The Globe and Mail*; and Royston James, "Tories deliver unkindest cut of all," *The Toronto Star* 3 December 1999.
46. Ontario Ministry of Municipal Affairs and Housing <http:/www.mmah.gov.on.ca/inthenews/backgrnd/19991202-2e.asp>

municipal government in Ottawa, Hamilton, Sudbury, and Haldimand-Norfolk, made relatively minor changes to the regional government systems in Halton and Waterloo, and extended the government's authority to 31 December 2002 to appoint commissioners with decision making authority to settle local restructuring disputes outside the areas covered by regional governments.

In explaining the legislation, Mr. Clement claimed that the legislation "generally follows the recommendations of the four Special Advisors."[47] These words were no doubt chosen carefully, because the government placed itself in a delicate position. On the one hand, it wanted to justify its actions on the basis of the special advisors' reports, especially since it wanted to claim that the solutions they recommended were in some sense locally derived. On the other, it wanted to show that it was sensitive to the requests of local Conservative MPPs and it wanted to avoid a situation in which the terms of the legislation would vary significantly for each area.

Opposition response focused on the fact that all the changes were implemented by a single bill that gave transition boards and the minister a great deal of regulatory authority. Such an approach enabled both opposition parties to oppose the bill, notwithstanding the fact that each contained members (including the Liberal leader himself) who represented centre-city constituencies and who personally favoured amalgamation. The media chose to highlight the government's decision not to accept Mr. Shortliffe's recommendation that the new city of Ottawa be declared officially bilingual. There was no reporting of the government's decision not to accept his recommendations that there be no police services board and no library board for the new city.

By looking at the bill alone, it is almost impossible to determine the government's policy with respect to the main principles structuring the amalgamations. It was clear, however, that the government decided not to allocate two votes to each of two rural councillors in the new city of Ottawa. Instead, it proposed a 21-member council having four rural wards, each with one councillor having one vote. The government's plan therefore violated the principle of representation-by-population just as much as Mr. Shortliffe's did.

The government's other decisions were communicated by press release, presumably to be implemented by the new regulatory authority granted the minister by the legislation. As far as financial arrangements are

---

47. Ontario, Ministry of Municipal Affairs and Housing, Press Release, "Legislation would lead to fewer politicians, lower taxes," 6 December 1999. <http://www.mmah.gov.on.ca/inthenews/releases/19991206-1e.asp>

concerned, a "backgrounder" for the press stated that "'The Special Advisors' recommendations with respect to area rating of services, liabilities and assets varied between the regions."[48] In principle, however, as we have seen, they did *not* vary. Each favoured area rating and the pooling of all assets and liabilities. However, the legislation gave the minister the authority to compel the new amalgamated municipalities to vary tax rates for the areas of the former municipalities for a period of up to eight years to take account of the different financial assets and liabilities that each former municipality brought to the new one. This provision enables the minister to force taxpayers in the old city of Ottawa to continue to pay back its debt and relieves the debt-free taxpayers of Nepean from bearing the burden. The provision has caused outrage among Ottawa centre-city politicians, who claim that the old city is bringing many valuable non-financial assets to the new city for which its taxpayers will receive no compensation.[49]

Significantly, there was no mention in any of the ministry's press releases about enforcing reductions in expenditures in the new municipalities or insisting on "average levelling" of salaries. Nor was there any indication that the minister gains any new authority to alter collective bargaining practices, except for certain temporary provisions during the actual period of transition in 2000.

The "backgrounders" for Ottawa and Hamilton did make specific reference to the minister's new authority "to initiate a process" whereby parts of the municipalities of West Carleton and Flamborough might be able to avoid being incorporated into the new cities of Ottawa and Hamilton respectively.[50] These arrangements were clearly concessions to the Conservative MPPs in whose constituencies these largely rural areas are located. In Flamborough's case, the MPP is Mr. Skarica, the one who promised in the 1999 election that no amalgamation would take place as long as he were in office.

The debate on the bill in the legislature provoked none of the passion associated with Toronto's megacity debate in 1997. In moving second reading, Mr. Clement emphasized the virtues of reducing the number of

---

48. Ontario, Ministry of Municipal Affairs and Housing, Backgrounder, "Ensuring Financial Protection for Taxpayers," 6 December 1999. <http://www.mmah.gov.on.ca/inthenews/backgrnd/19991206-6e.asp>

49. 48Randall Denley, "How to deal fairly with Ottawa's debt," *The Ottawa Citizen*, 13 December 1999.

50. Ontario, Ministry of Municipal Affairs and Housing, Backgrounders, "The City of Ottawa" and "The City of Hamilton," 6 December 1999. <http://www.mmah.gov.on.ca/inthenews/backgrnd/19991206-4e.asp>, <http://www./gov.on.ca/inthe news/backgrnd/19991206-3e.asp>

municipal politicians and of saving money. In his account of projected savings, he included savings that had *already* been achieved in Hamilton-Wentworth by merging the administrations of the city and the region, and he included the projected "efficiency" savings in Ottawa, savings that were not directly attributable to the amalgamation.[51] He made no attempt to explain why or how the terms of the legislation differed from what was recommended by the special advisors. During the debate, one of Mr. Clement's cabinet colleagues – John Baird, the MPP from Nepean-Carleton – was less reluctant to address such issues. After proudly reviewing his own role in the debate, Mr. Baird concluded:

> I do want to thank my friend and colleague the Honourable Tony Clement, someone whom I have known for more than 15 years, for listening and for agreeing to major departures from the Shortliffe report. This bill is not perfect – as I've said, it's not my first choice – but Bill 25 is a major improvement from the report of the special adviser.[52]

Another of Mr. Clement's cabinet colleagues, the MPP from Lanark-Carleton, traced the cause of the amalgamation to the previous NDP government:

> This whole notion towards going away from a two-tier system to a one-tier system started in 1994, when the then NDP government forced upon the region the withdrawal of the local mayors from regional council. That was really the beginning of the end of the two-tier system of government at the regional level in Ottawa-Carleton, because essentially what happened was that a lack of trust built up between the 11 lower-tier mayors and the upper-tier council. As a result of that, along with the direct election of the regional chair, giving him much more power in a political sense in terms of who was behind him, we really saw at that point in time the death of the lower-tier governments in Ottawa-Carleton.[53]

The legislation received third reading on 20 December 1999. Because it was not sent to committee, amendments could not be proposed; nor could there be public hearings. Much of the opposition members' speeches were directed against such hasty procedures. The government's response was that all these issues had been studied for years and that the special advisors were the ones charged with conducting the public hearings. Two

---

51. Ontario, Legislative Assembly, *Hansard*, 13 December 1999.
52. Ontario, *Hansard*, 14 December 1999.
53. Ontario, *Hansard*, 14 December 1999.

suburban Hamilton MPPs, including Mr. Skarica, voted against the bill. But even Mr. Skarica did not speak to the legislature about his reasons for opposing amalgamation; he referred only to the need for politicians to keep their word.[54]

Conclusion

As we have seen in earlier chapters of this report, past debates about municipal amalgamation, even in Ontario, have involved serious consideration of important issues: regional planning, city-suburban equity, the difficulties of choosing (in some circumstances at least) between the benefits of being small and the benefits of being big. In Toronto's megacity debate, these issues were at least aired, although many claimed that the government refused to listen. In December 1999, when new single-tier amalgamated cities were created for Ottawa, Hamilton, and Sudbury, the debate seemed over before it had begun. Had any one of the special advisors in these three areas recommended anything other than complete amalgamation, municipal observers would have been shocked. Almost as soon as the special advisors were appointed, the media started referring to them as the "amalgamation advisors."

When a provincial government's main objective is to reduce the number of municipal politicians, it can achieve its objective by: 1) amalgamating municipalities; and/or 2) legislating a reduction in council size. The *Fewer Municipal Politicians Act, 1999* adopts both strategies. The end result was 203 fewer municipal politicians. For policy makers in other jurisdictions who wish to reduce the number of local politicians, Ontario's *Fewer Municipal Politicians Act, 1999* no doubt merits emulation. Similarly, other Canadian provincial governments intent on maintaining control of their most powerful and populous municipalities can no doubt learn much from what the government of Ontario has done to Toronto's city council. But anyone concerned with the effective governance of complex city-regions in the early 21st century has little to learn from events in Ontario in late 1999.

---

54. Ontario, *Hansard*, 13 December 1999. True to his word, Mr. Skarika resigned from the legislature in January 2000.

CONCLUSION

WHAT PROBLEMS IN MONTREAL ARE MUNICIPAL AMALGAMATIONS SUPPOSED TO SOLVE?

A s noted in the Introduction, no one in Montreal advocates merging all of the metropolitan region's 111 muni-cipalities into one gigantic municipality. The largest proposed amal-gamation involves all 28 municipalities that make up the territory of the Montreal Urban Community. Such a new city would lack the territorial comprehensiveness favoured by so many of the most fervent advocates of consolidation. Of the amalgamations discussed in this report, the ones in Philadelphia, New York, Winnipeg, and Halifax all were designed to create a single municipality for a single city-region. (This also applies to the recent decisions in Ontario concerning amalgamations in Ottawa-Carleton, Hamilton-Wentworth, and Sudbury.)

When consolidationists realized that the single-municipality solution was not possible in most places, they tended to adopt a two-tier solution of the type epitomized by the Greater London Council (1965-86) and Municipality of Metropolitan Toronto (1954-97). As we have seen, the GLC was abolished by the Thatcher government and is being replaced – in a much lighter form and without any lower-tier amalgamations – by the Blair government. In Toronto, the two-tier Metro system has been replaced by the megacity. In most parts of the world, two-tier systems have recently come under considerable attack for being too cumbersome and conflictual, although in the United States many people are now looking more favourably on the two-tier systems that exist in Miami-Dade County, Florida and in Portland, Oregon.[1] In neither of these cases has the establishment of an upper-tier level of municipal government been accompanied by

---

1. G. Ross Stephens and Nelson Wikstrom, *Metropolitan Government and Governance: Theoretical Perspectives, Empirical Analysis, and the Future* (New York: Oxford University Press, 2000), pp.88-95 and 99-101.

municipal amalgamations. Indeed, one of the main reasons for establishing an upper tier in the first place is to capture the benefits of large-scale institutions while still enabling smaller ones to carry on for other purposes.

Mayor Bourque's proposal to amalgamate all the MUC municipalities bears some resemblance to the Ontario government's megacity policy for Toronto. In both cases a large, dominant central-city municipality would be formed within an even larger city-region. Mayor Bourque advocates enlarging the MUC (but without a policing function), thereby creating a relatively strong upper-tier government for the entire Montreal metropolitan region. Ironically, if the Harris government had been willing to establish such an upper-tier authority for the Greater Toronto Area (i.e. following the recommendations of the Golden task force), it is highly unlikely it ever would have adopted a megacity policy. For the Harris government, large-scale amalgamation resulted from its rejection of a new, territorially enlarged upper-tier authority. But Mayor Bourque seems to want large-scale amalgamation *and* a strong upper-tier authority. The great weakness in both Mayor Bourque's position and that of the Harris government, is that neither is able to show how the creation of one overwhelmingly dominant municipality within a city-region is likely to enhance inter-municipal regional co-operation, with or without a powerful upper-tier council. This is a serious weakness, because all the studies of municipal problems in the GTA and in Greater Montreal have pointed to the urgent need to promote such co-operation, not to establish a giant central city.

There are three important differences in the governmental and political environment in the pre-megacity Toronto city-region and in today's Montreal city-region:

1. The city of Montreal (population 1.0 million) is already more dominant within the Montreal Urban Community (1.8 million) than the old city of Toronto (0.7 million) was within Metro (2.4 million). This no doubt explains why the old city of Toronto was a fervent opponent of Toronto's megacity while the current city of Montreal favours a megacity for Montreal. One of the central motivations of the Harris government was to eliminate the political and administrative extravagances that it perceived in the old city of Toronto. It is, however, hard to see how an amalgamated MUC would be anything other than a complete takeover by the city of Montreal. Regardless of whether or not a Montreal takeover would be good public policy, everyone should at least acknowledge that such an end result is the exact opposite of what the megacity in Toronto was all about.

2. There were six constituent municipalities in Metro Toronto. There are 28 in the MUC. The complexities and expenses of the Toronto amalgamation would seem minor in comparison to a Montreal amalgamation. For example, all municipal employees in Ontario belong to one pension plan, the Ontario Municipal Employee Retirement System (OMERS). Within the MUC, each municipality has its own pension plan. Arranging retirement packages and standardizing pension arrangements after an MUC amalgamation would be an administrative and financial nightmare. The only way to simplify the transition in Montreal would be to eliminate the suburban work forces and to let the city of Montreal administrative procedures and practices be established everywhere. The result of such a policy would be to guarantee significant increases in costs and to challenge severely the city of Montreal's management capacity.

3. Municipal political parties were not – and are not – a factor in Toronto. In the MUC they exist in some municipalities and not in others. It is hard to imagine that they would not exist in an amalgamated island city. Has anyone given any thought to the implications of establishing a single municipal party system throughout a Montreal megacity? Surely one result would be that many people who currently are willing to serve on suburban municipal councils would be less likely to run for office. Or perhaps the current parties would be relatively weaker within the new council. Has anyone thought about how the new city council would function in the absence of a majority party? Will a new mayor of an amalgamated Montreal ever be in as strong a political position as Mel Lastman has been in Toronto?

It is extremely difficult to understand the arguments in favour of an amalgamated MUC. In Toronto, the provincial government wanted to get rid of one tier of directly elected municipal government. This is not an issue in Montreal, because MUC councillors have never been directly elected to serve only at that level. Saving money appears not to be a strong motivating factor in Montreal. In any event, experience in Toronto and elsewhere should quickly disabuse anyone of the notion that an amalgamation on this scale will save money.[2] Similarly, no one in Quebec

2. On this topic for Montreal, see the Municonsult study for the Union des Municipalités de Banlieue sur l'île de Montréal: "Les Regroupements municipaux sur l'île de Montréal, " October 1999, pp.16-31. See also, Québec, *Pacte 2000: Rapport de la commission nationale sur les finances et la fiscalité locales* (Québec: Les Publications du Québec, 1999) p.266 and Jacques Desbiens, *Fusions municipales et économies d'échelle: mythes et réalités* (Chicoutimi: Le groupe Jacques Desbiens, 1999).

seems as concerned as the Harris government ever was about reducing the number of elected politicians. Does anyone seriously believe that members of councils for suburban municipalities within the MUC are somehow a drain on the public purse?

Arguments based on concerns about economic development miss the point. If they were relevant, they would apply to the entire city-region. Of course, there is a need to promote Montreal throughout the world. But *all* municipalities in the region should be involved, not just those on the island of Montreal. As countless American city-regions have proved, city-regions can grow, prosper, and breed innovation when there are dozens or even hundreds of municipalities. Municipal amalgamation has nothing to do with economic development.[3]

Social equity is another prominent argument. No one wants to promote or defend a system of municipal government that favours the rich and places undue burdens on the poor. Unlike the situation in Ontario, Quebec municipalities have virtually no role in social services and none in relation to income security. Wealthy Montrealers cannot escape paying for social services and welfare by moving to a suburb. Apparently, however, the city of Montreal spends $9.3 million annually on social housing. Its total operating budget in 1999 was $1.821 billion.[4] Social housing therefore constitutes 0.5 per cent of its annual expenditures. If this is the source of the city's financial difficulties, it would appear that the problem could be solved without amalgamation. We must realize that because the MUC already exists and acts as a mechanism for sharing central-city police costs, and because the province finances social services and income security, the city of Montreal probably bears fewer costs of central-city poverty than almost any other such major central city in North America.

If the claim is really that the city provides all kinds of services to commuters, then we become involved in an unending debate about city-suburban benefits and burdens, a debate that has been going on for decades everywhere in North America and wherever municipalities tax local residents and businesses for local public services. The debate is probably unresolvable.[5] It is likely, however, that most central cities lose

3. I expand on this point in "Globalization Does Not Require Amalgamation," Policy Options, 20-9 (November 1999), 54-58 and in "Jane Jacobs on the Organization of Municipal Government," *Journal of Urban Affairs*, forthcoming in Vol.22, No.4.
4. Ville de Montréal, *One Island, One City: For a Strong Metropolis* (1999). For a two-paragraph description in the Bédard report which says nothing about actual programs delivered by the city of Montreal, see Québec, *Pacte 2000*, pp.185-6.
5. For a discussion, see Québec, *Pacte 2000*, pp.175-6 and 202-3.

more than they gain from commuters. But, once again, because the MUC covers policing costs, the burden borne by the city of Montreal is significantly reduced, if not eliminated.

We are left with arguments for amalgamation that are essentially little more than appeals to municipal grandeur (in the case of Mayor Bourque) or administrative tidiness (in the case of the Bédard report).[6] We know that municipal boundaries in Montreal (and most other places) appear strange when seen on a map. We know that people cross them all the time without thinking. We know that some municipalities are much bigger than others. But anyone who wants to change such boundaries against the will of the people affected should be obliged to specify the precise problem or problems for which the boundary change is the solution. The difficulty in confronting the case for municipal amalgamation within the MUC is that the problems that are allegedly to be corrected have not been specified.

Mayor Bourque has spoken and written frequently about the desirability of amalgamation.[7] On some occasions he has made specific reference to developments elsewhere. For example on 24 November 1999 he wrote the following in *The Gazette*:

> We cannot deny that we are influenced by events elsewhere in Canada. We cannot ignore the fact that mergers are taking place in Ontario and Nova Scotia. Toronto has a population of 2.4 million and Halifax close to 400,000. Even now, the Ontario government is planning additional amalgamations in Ottawa and Hamilton regions as well as in other areas. If consolidation works for Toronto and Halifax, and is being considered for Ottawa, why wouldn't it work for Montreal, Quebec City, and Sherbrooke? Are we that different? Do we live in another economic world? Does disunity foster strength, as some would have us believe?

The object of this report has been to enable us to place such comments in perspective.

We know from this report that most Canadian provinces and most advanced liberal democracies – especially the United States and countries in continental Europe – are *not* now absorbed in merger mania. It is particularly notable that American cities are now receiving substantial amounts of assistance from federal and state governments to rebuild their infrastructure at the same time as they have forged partnerships with the private sector and with philanthropical foundations to start rejuvenating

---

6. For the Bédard report, see Québec, *Pacte 2000*, pp.275-6
7. The city's case is presented on its website. See <http:www.ville.montreal.qc.ca/uneile_uneville/english/une00e.htm>

their inner cities. Regional thinking dominates in such endeavours. But it is all being done without municipal amalgamations.

We also know that it is far from clear that "consolidation works for Toronto and Halifax." Most Haligonians, as we have seen, would dispute such a claim. Business interests are supportive of the amalgamation because they think it favours economic development. But the notion that investors favour single-municipality city-regions has not been proven. Given the reality in North America as a whole, it scarcely seems credible. Torontonians appear to support amalgamation because their taxes have remained steady and they have been told that it is saving money. This report has shown that is far too early to arrive at such optimistic conclusions.

The overarching purpose of this report has been to demonstrate that people in various democratic countries have been thinking and acting on proposals for municipal amalgamation for at least a century and a half. There are no new arguments. Even the claim that globalization requires amalgamation is simply a variation of an old argument that was advanced during the consolidation debates in New York more than 100 years ago. The only difference is that the argument was probably more valid then than it is now. Municipalities 100 years ago were relatively much more functionally powerful and important in relation to state and federal governments than they are currently.

It is, of course, true – as the proponents of amalgamation constantly point out – that cities have grown dramatically in importance over the past century. It is probably more true in Quebec than just about anywhere else. But just because *cities* are increasingly the places where our economic growth and wealth are generated does not mean that *municipalities* have grown correspondingly in importance. In fact, the opposite is the case. Municipalities in North America carry on doing much the same sorts of things they did a hundred years ago: they provide the basic public infrastructure and services that make life in a city possible. They used to be – together with charities – solely responsible for the well-being of their poor. Fortunately, this is no longer the case in most places, certainly not in Montreal.

Throughout much of Europe, including Britain, municipalities have become the mechanisms through which the central government provides such labour-intensive and redistributive services such as public education, day care, social services, services for the aged, and some aspects of health care. In these countries, almost all teachers and social workers are employed directly by municipal governments, even if much of the policy-making and financing comes from the centre. In these circumstances, it is not surprising that central governments are concerned that sometimes municipalities are too small to deliver all the required services. But amalgamation is not always the desired solution even in these circumstances, as experience in France so readily demonstrates. In North America – especially Quebec – where municipalities focus primarily on services to property, what are the services that require a municipality to have a population beyond a certain specified number? It is true that some services – water supply and sewage treatment for example – *are* often more efficiently delivered over a large urban territory than a small one. But other services – recreation programs, fire suppression, and police patrol – suffer from diseconomies of scale. Why would we always want to amalgamate to accommodate some services rather than stay small to accommodate others?

In the real world, such choices are not even necessary. Small municipalities can contract with larger organizations, both public and private, to provide services that are most efficiently delivered over larger territories. It would perhaps be reassuring to know that large municipalities could decentralize themselves – both politically and administratively – so that they could capture the benefits of smallness. Unfortunately, experience in Canada and elsewhere with various forms of community committees and councils has not been sustainable or especially satisfactory. Perhaps the "Unigov" system in Indianapolis comes closest to the model of a genuinely decentralized amalgamated government. But it is so decentralized – even while excluding some municipalities whose territory it surrounds – that, by Canadian standards, it hardly qualifies as an amalgamation.

Municipalities are more than just providers of services. They are the democratic mechanisms through which territorially based communities of people govern themselves at a local level. Almost everyone agrees that such forms of government are crucial components of our liberal democracies. Those who would force municipalities to amalgamate with each other invariably claim that their motive is to make municipalities stronger. In most cases, they are perfectly sincere in expressing such a motive. But deeper reflection suggests that the message they are really delivering is something quite different. The real message is that local communities of citizens are incapable of knowing their own best interests while those at the centre know what is best. Such an approach – however well-intentioned – erodes the foundations of our liberal democracies because it undermines the notion that there can be forms of self-government that exist outside the institutions of the central government (or governments, in the case of federal systems).

Municipal autonomy is never absolute, nor should it be. Many central rules and regulations for municipalities are quite routine and completely justified. But as we progress along the scale of central intervention to the point where it is contemplated that entire municipal governments might be abolished without local approval, then surely the standards that justify such drastic action become more demanding. Advocates of coerced municipal amalgamation are obliged to state clearly exactly how and why they think amalgamation will benefit the wider public interest. Their claims can more effectively be evaluated if we know something about what has happened when such amalgamations have been advocated and implemented elsewhere in similar, but never identical, circumstances. This report has been written to assist in such a process.

BIBLIOGRAPHY

ALBERTA, Alberta Capital Region Review <http://www.acrgr.org/default.cfm>

ALLEN, Oliver E., *New York, New York* (New York: Athaneum, 1990)

ANDERSSON, David E., "Regions and the Collectivity: Swedish Local Government and the Case of Stockholm" in A.E. Andersson, B. Harsman, and J.M. Quigley, eds., *Governments for the Future - Unification, Fragmentation and Regionalism* (Elsevier Science, 1997)

ATKINSON, Hugh, "New Labour, New Local Government?" in Gerald R. Taylor, ed., *The Impact of New Labour* (Basingstoke, Hampshire, Macmillan, 1999)

AXWORTHY, Lloyd, "The Best Laid Plans Oft Go Astray: The Case of Winnipeg," in M.O. Dickerson, S. Drabek and J.T. Woods (eds.), *Problems of Change in Urban Government* (Waterloo ON: Wilfrid Laurier University Press, 1980)

BEERS, Dorothy Gondos, "The Centennial City, 1865-1876" in Russell. F. Weigley, ed., *Philadelphia: A 300-Year History* (New York: W.W. Norton, 1982)

BISH, Robert L. and Vincent OSTROM, *Understanding Urban Government: Metropolitan Reform Reconsidered* (Washington DC: American Enterprise Institute for Public Policy Research, 1973)

BLOMQUIST, William and Roger B. PARKS, "Unigov: Local Government in Indianapolis and Marion County, Indiana," in L.J. Sharpe, ed. *The Government of World Cities: The Future of the Metro Model* (Chichester, England: John Wiley and Sons, 1995)

BOURQUE, Pierre, "Time for a common vision," *The Gazette*, 24 November 1999

BOYNE, George, "Population Size and Economies of Scale in Local Government," *Policy and Politics*, 23-3 (1995), 213-22

BROWNSTONE, Meyer and T.J. PLUNKETT, *Metropolitan Winnipeg: Politics and Reform of Local Government* (Berkeley: University of California Press, 1983)

BUSH, Graham, *Local Government and Politics in New Zealand*, 2nd ed. (Auckland: Auckland University Press, 1995)

CANADA, *Census of Canada*, (various years)

CARO, Robert A., *The Power Broker: Robert Moses and the Fall of New York* (New York: Alfred A. Knopf, 1974)

CHARTRAND, Luc, "Villes: fusions attention!" *l'Actualité*, 1 November 1999, pp.19-20

COLLIN, Jean-Pierre, "Les Stratégies fiscales municipales et la gestion de l'agglomération urbaine: le cas de la ville de Montréal entre 1910 et 1965," *Urban History Review/Revue d'Histoire Urbaine* 23-1 (November 1993-4), pp.19-31

COLTON, Timothy J., *Big Daddy: Frederick G. Gardiner and the Building of Metropolitan Toronto* (Toronto: University of Toronto Press, 1980)

CORPORATION OF THE CITY OF SCARBOROUGH V. ATTORNEY GENERAL FOR ONTARIO, 24 February 1997 <http://community.web.net/citizens/103Updates/feb24.html>

DANIELSON, Michael N. and Jameson W. DOIG, *New York: The Politics of Urban Regional Development* (Berkeley: University of California Press, 1982)

DEARLOVE, John, *The Reorganisation of British Local Government: Old Orthodoxies and a Political Perspective* (London: Cambridge University Press, 1979)

DESBIENS, Jacques, *Fusions municipales et économies d'échelle: mythes et réalités* (Chicoutimi: Le groupe Jacques Desbiens, 1999)

DODGE, William R., *Regional Excellence: Governing Together to Compete Globally and Flourish Locally* (Washington DC: National League of Cities, 1996)

DOMINION BOND RATING SERVICE, "Bond, Long Term Debt & Preferred Share Ratings: City of Toronto," 16 December 1998

DOWNEY, Terrence J. and Robert J. WILLIAMS, "Provincial Agendas, Local Responses: The 'Common Sense' Restructuring of Ontario's Municipal Governments," *Canadian Public Administration*, 41-2 (Summer 1998)

EAST YORK (BOROUGH) v. ONTARIO (1997) 153 D.L.R. (4th) 299 (Ont. C.A.)

FOSTER, Kathryn A., "Exploring the Links Between Political Structure and Economic Growth," *Political Geography*, 12-6 (1993), 523-47

FRISKEN, Frances, "The Greater Toronto Area in Transition: The Search for New Planning and Servicing Strategies" in Donald N. Rothblatt and Andrew Sancton, eds., *Metropolitan Governance Revisited: American/Canadian Intergovernmental Perspectives* (Berkeley: Institute of Governmental Studies Press at the University of California, 1998), pp.161-235

FUCHS, Esther R., *Mayors and Money: Fiscal Policy in New York and Chicago* (Chicago: University of Chicago Press, 1992)

GARCEA, Joseph, "Saskatchewan's Aborted Municipal Service Districts Act (Bill33): Pegasus or Trojan Horse," paper presented to the annual meeting of the Canadian Political Science association, St. John's, Newfoundland, June 1997

GEFFEN, Elizabeth M., "Industrial Development and Social Crisis, 1841-1854," in Russell. F. Weigley, ed., *Philadelphia: A 300-Year History* (New York: W.W. Norton, 1982)

GLOBE & MAIL (Toronto)

HALIFAX CHRONICLE-HERALD

171

HALIFAX REGIONAL MUNICIPALITY, *HRM Access and Information Guide*, no date

HALIFAX THIS WEEK <http://novanewsnet.ukings.ns.ca/stories/96-97/ 970314 amalgamation.htm>

HAMILTON SPECTATOR

HAMMACK, David C., *Power and Society: Greater New York at the Turn of the Century* (New York: Russell Sage Foundation, 1982)

HARRIGAN John J., *Political Change in the Metropolis*, 5th ed. (New York: HarperCollins, 1993)

HORAK, Martin, "The Power of Local Identity: C4LD and the Anti-amalgamation Mobilization in Toronto," Research Paper 195, Centre for Urban and Conmmunity Studies at the University of Toronto, November 1998

IBBITSON, John, *Promised Land: Inside the Mike Harris Revolution* (Toronto, Prentice-Hall, 1997)

JEZIERSKI, Louise, "Pittsburgh: Partnerships in a Regional City" in H.V. Savitch and Ronald K. Vogel, eds, *Regional Politics: America in a Post-City Age*, Urban Affairs Annual Reviews 45, Thousand Oaks CA: SAGE, 1996)

JONES, Victor, *Metropolitan Government* (Chicago: University of Chicago Press, 1942)

KPMG, *Fresh Start: An Estimate of Potential savings and Costs from the Creation of Single Tier Local Government for Toronto*, 16 December 1996

KPMG OTTAWA, "Project Report: Ottawa-Carleton Restructuring Options - A Financial Analysis," prepared for the regional Municipality of Ottawa-Carleton, 25 August 1999

KINGDOM, John, "Centralisation and Fragmentation: John Major and the Reform of Local Government" in Peter Dorey, ed., *The Major*

Premiership: Politics and Policies under John Major, 1990-97 (Basingstoke, Hampshire: Macmillan, 1999)

KINGSTON/FRONTENAC/LENNOX AND ADDINGTON GOVERNANCE REVIEW COMMITTEE, "Proposal for the Reform of Local Governance: Kingston/Frontenac," 10 July 1996

KISS, Rosemary, "Local Government to Local Administration," in Brian Costar and Nick Economou, eds. *The Kennett Revolution: Victorian Politics in the 1990s* (Sydney: University of New South Wales Press, 1999)

KITCHEN, Harry, "Ontario: Municipal Funding Responsibilities and Governing Structure at the Millenium," paper presented to AMO - Regions and Counties, Ottawa, 25 October 1999

KLAUSEN, Kurt Klaudi, "Danish Local Government: Integrating into the EU?" in M.J.F. Goldsmith and K.K. Klausen, eds., *European Integration and Local Government* (Cheltenham: Edward Elgar, 1997

KNOX, Paul L. and Peter J. TAYLOR, eds., *World Cities in a World System* (Cambridge: Cambridge University Press, 1995)

KULISEK, Larry and Trevor PRICE, "Ontario Municipal Policy Affecting Local Autonomy: A Case Study Involving Windsor and Toronto," *Urban History Review,* 16-3 (February 1988), 255-70

KUSHNER, Joseph, Isodore MASSE, Thomas PETERS, and Lewis SOROKA, "The Determinants of Municipal Expenditures in Ontario," *Canadian Tax Journal,* 44-2 (1996), 451-64

LEACH, Steve and Gerry STOKER, "Understanding the Local Government Review: A Retrospective Analysis," *Public Administration,* 75 (Spring 1997)

LEMIEUX, Julie, "Fusions municipales," *Le Soleil,* 28 & 29 October 1999

LOCAL GOVERNMENT AND SHIRES ASSOCIATIONS (New South Wales, Australia) <http://www.lsga.org.au/web.councils.nsf/Listing>

LONDON FREE PRESS

LORINC, John, "The Making of the Megacity," *Toronto Life*, November 1998

LORINC, John, "Scarborough Toughs," *Toronto Life*, January 1999

LORINC, John, "Rail to the Chief," *Toronto Life*, April 1999

LORINC, John, "Harmonize This," *Toronto Life*, June 1999

MALENFANT, J.E. Louis and John C. ROBISON, *Greater Moncton Urban community: Strength through Cooperation* (Fredericton: Ministry of Municipalities, Culture and Housing, 1994)

MANITOBA, *Proposals for Urban Reorganization in the Greater Winnipeg Area* (1970)

MANITOBA, Committee of Review, City of Winnipeg Act, *Report and Recommendations* (Winnipeg: Queen's Printer for Manitoba, 1976)

MANITOBA, City of Winnipeg Act Review Committee, *Final Report 1986*

MANITOBA, Ministry of Urban Affairs, *Annual Report 1991-92*

MANITOBA, Capital Region Review, *Partners for the Future: Working Together to Strengthen Manitoba's Capital Region* (1998), p.3. <http:www.susdev.gov.mb.ca/capreg/crpub.html

MANITOBA, Capital Region Review, *Interim Panel Report*, 15 July 1999 <http:www.susdev.gov.mb.ca/interimreport/index.html>

MARSAN, Jean-Claude, *Montreal in Evolution: Historical Analysis of the Development of Montreal's Architecture and Urban Environment* (Montreal: McGill-Queen's University Press, 1981)

MARTIN, Judith J., "Renegotiating Metropolitan Consciousness: The Twin Cities Faces its Future," in Donald N. Rothblatt and Andrew Sancton, eds. *Metropolitan Governance Revisited: Canadian-American Intergovernmental Perspectives* (Berkeley: Institute of Governmental Studies Press at the University of California, 1998)

MEECH, Ken R. and Rudy VODICKA, "Hindsight is 20/20: Planning for Amalgamation in the Halifax Regional Municipality," *Cordillera Institute Journal*, 1-1(1997)

MELLON, Hugh, "Reforming the Electoral System of Metropolitan Toronto: Doing Away with Dual representation," *Canadian Public Administration*, 36-1 (Spring 1993), 38-56

MEYNAUD, Jean and Jacques LÉVEILLÉE, *La régionalisation municipale au Québec* (Montreal: Editions Nouvelle Frontière, 1973)

MILLWARD, Hughand Shelley DICKEY, "Industrial Decentralization and the Planned Industrial Park: A Case Study of Metropolitan Halifax" in Frances Frisken, ed., *The Changing Canadian Metropolis: A Public Policy Perspective* (Berkeley CA: Institute of Governmental Studies Press at the University of California, 1994), pp.751-76

MONTGOMERY, Byron J., *Annexation and Restructuring in Sarnia-Lambton: A Model for Ontario County Government?* Local Government Case Studies #4 (London, Ontario: University of Western Ontario Department of Political Science, 1991)

MONTRÉAL, *One Island, One City: For a Strong Metropolis* (1999)

MORRIS, Charles R., *The Cost of Good Intentions: New York City and the Liberal Intentions, 1960 - 1975* (New York: W.W. Norton, 1980)

MUNICONSULT, "Les Regroupements municipaux sur l'île de Montréal, " October 1999

MUNRO, W.B., *American Influences on Canadian Government* (Toronto: Macmillan, 1929)

NATIONAL POST

NELSON, M.A., "Municipal Amalgamation and the Growth of the Local Public Sector in Sweden," *Journal of Regional Science*, 32 (1992)

NORTON, Alan, *International Handbook of Local and Regional Government: A Comparative Analysis of Advanced Democracies* (Aldershot, Hants.: Edward Elgar, 1994)

175

NOVA SCOTIA, Royal Commission on on Education, Public Services and Provincial-Municipal Relations, *Report* (Halifax: Queen's Printer, 1974)

NOVA SCOTIA, Task Force on Local Government, *Report to the Government of Nova Scotia*, April 1992

NOVA SCOTIA, Municipal Affairs, *Interim Report of the Implementation Commissioner, Cape Breton County*, 1993

NOVA SCOTIA, Municipal Affairs, *Interim Report of the Municipal Reform Commissioner, Halifax County (Halifax Metropolitan Area)*, 1993

OAKERSON, Ronald J., *Governing Local Public Economies: Creating the Civic Metropolis* (San Francisco: Institute for Contemporary Studies Press, 1999)

O'BRIEN, Allan, *Municipal Consolidation in Canada and its Alternatives* (Toronto: ICURR Press, 1993)

ONTARIO, Legislative Assembly, *Hansard*

ONTARIO, *Report of the Royal Commission on Metropolitan Toronto* (1965)

ONTARIO, "Statement by the Honourable John Robarts, Prime Minister of Ontario, Re Report of the Royal Commission on Mteropolitan Toronto," 10 January, 1966

ONTARIO, Municipal Affairs, Lakehead Local Government Review, *Report and Recommendations* (1968)

ONTARIO, Municipal Affairs, Waterloo Area Local Government Review, *Report* (1970)

ONTARIO, *Report of the Royal Commission on Metropolitan Toronto*, 2 vols. (1977)

ONTARIO, Ontario, *Report of the Hamilton-Wentworth Review Commission* (1978)

ONTARIO, Intergovernmental Affairs, *Report of the Waterloo Region Review Commission* (1979)

ONTARIO, Municipal Affairs, Consultation Committee to the Minister, *County Government in Ontario*, (January 1989)

ONTARIO, Municipal Affairs, *Toward an Ideal County* (January 1990)

ONTARIO, Municipal Affairs, News releases <http://www.mmah.gov.on.ca/inthnews/releases>

ONTARIO, Task Force on the Future of the Greater Toronto Area, *Greater Toronto: Report of the GTA Task Force* (Toronto: Queen's Printer, 1996)

ONTARIO, Municipal Affairs, County of Kent and City of Chatham Restructuring Commission, *Final Restructuring Proposal for Kent County and the City of Chatham and Order of the Commission*, 28 April 1997

ONTARIO, Municipal Affairs and Housing, "Report of the Special Advisor, Haldimand-Norfolk Review, Milt Farrow," November 1999

ONTARIO, Municipal Affairs and Housing, "Report to the Minister: Local Government Reform in the Regional Municipality of Ottawa-Carleton," 25 November 1999

ONTARIO PROGRESSIVE CONSERVATIVE CAUCUS, "News Release -- Mike Harris: Bringing Common sense to Metro Government" 5 January 1995

ORFIELD, Myron, *Metropolitics: A Regional Agenda for Community and Stability*, rev. ed. (Washington DC: Brookings Institution Press, 1997)

OSTROM, Vincent, Robert BISH, and Elinor OSTROM, *Local Government in the United States* (San Francisco: Institute for Contemporary Studies Press, 1988)

OTTAWA CITIZEN

PARKIN, Andrew, *Governing the Cities: The Australian Experience in Perspective* (South Melbourne, Macmillan of Australia, 1982)

PEIRCE, Neal R. *Citistates: How Urban America Can Prosper in a Competitive World* (Washington DC: Seven Locks Press, 1993)

PENDERGRAST, Eudora and John FARROW, *Community Councils and Neighbourhood Committees: Lessons for our Communities from around the World* (Toronto: Canadian Urban Institute, 1997)

PETERSON, Paul E. *City Limits* (Chicago: University of Chicago Press, 1981)

POEL, Dale H., "[Not] Thinking Regionally: Citizen Responses to Municipal Consolidation," a paper presented at the annual meeting of the Canadian Regional Science Association, Montreal, November 1999

POEL, Dale H. and Ruth BRUER, "The Consequences of Amalgamation: Setting the Research Agenda for the HRM Project," paper presented to the CAPPA/IPAC annual conference, Montreal, August 1998

PRICE WATERHOUSE, *The Municipalities of Ottawa-Carleton: Study of the Financial Impact of One-Tier Government in Ottawa-Carleton*, 27 August 1992

PROGRESSIVE CONSERVATIVE PARTY OF ONTARIO, *The Common Sense Revolution*, 1994

PROGRESSIVE CONSERVATIVE PARTY OF ONTARIO, *Blueprint*, 1999

QUEBEC, l'Assemblée legislative, *Débats*

QUEBEC, Ministry of Municipal Affairs, *Study Commission of Intermunicipal Problems on the Island of Montreal* (Quebec: Queen's Printer, 1964)

QUEBEC, Ministère des affaires municipales, Commission d'étude sur les problèmes intermunicipaux de l'Ile Jésus, *Rapport final* (1964)

QUEBEC, Ministère de l'Industrie et du Commerce, Bureau de la statistique du Québec, *Finances municipales por l'année terminée le 30 avril 1966* (1966)

QUEBEC, Ministère des affaires municipales, *Finances des organismes municipaux pour l'exercise financier 1996* (Quebec: les Publications du Québec, 1998)

QUEBEC, Quebec, *Pacte 2000: Rapport de la Commission nationale sur les finances et la fiscalité locales* (1999)

RHODES, Gerald, *The Government of London: The Struggle for Reform* (Toronto: University of Toronto Press, 1970)

ROBISON, John C., "Public Participation in Restructuring Local Government to Create the City of Miramichi" in K.A. Graham and S.D. Phillips, eds., *Citizen Engagement: Lessons in Participation from Local Government* (Toronto: Institute of Public Administration of Canada, 1998)

ROSE, Albert, *Governing Metropolitan Toronto: A Social and Political Analysis, 1953-1971* (Berkeley: University of California Press, 1972)

RUSK, David, *Cities Without Suburbs*, 2nd ed. (Washington DC: Woodrow Wilson Center Press, 1995)

SAINT JOHN TIMES-GLOBE

SANCTON, Andrew, *Governing the Island of Montreal: Language differences and Metropolitan Politics* (Berkeley: University of California Press, 1983)

SANCTON, Andrew, "Mayors as Political Leaders" in Maureen Mancuso, Richard G. Price, and Ronald Wagenberg, eds., *Leaders and Leadership in Canada* (Toronto: Oxford University Press, 1994), pp. 174-89

SANCTON, Andrew, Sancton, *Governing Canada's City-Regions* (Montreal: Institute for Research on Public Policy, 1994)

SANCTON, Andrew, "Assessing the GTA Task Force's proposals on Governance," *Policy Options*, September 1996, pp.38-41

SANCTON, Andrew, "Reducing Costs by Consolidating Municipalities: New Brunswick, Nova Scotia, Ontario," *Canadian Public Administration*, 39-3 (Fall 1996), 267-89

SANCTON, Andrew, "Toronto's Response to the KPMG Report," 17 December 1996

SANCTON, Andrew, "Introduction" in Donald N. Rothblatt and Andrew Sancton, eds. *Metropolitan Governance Revisted* (Berlekey: Institute of Governmental Studies Press at the University of California, 1998)

SANCTON, Andrew, "Negotiating, Arbitrating, Legislating: Where was the Public in London's Boundary Adjustment?" in K.A. Graham and S.D. Phillips, eds., *Citizen Engagement: Lessons in Participation from Local Government* (Toronto: Institute of Public Administration of Canada, 1998)

SANCTON, Andrew, "Globalization Does Not Require Amalgamation," *Policy Options*, 20-9 (November 1999), 54-58

SELF, Peter, "The Future of Australian Local Government" in Brian Dollery and Neil Marshall, eds., *Australian Local Government: Reform and Renewal* (Melbourne: Macmillan Education Australia, 1997)

SHARPE, L.J., "Local Government Reorganization: General Theory and UK Practice" in Bruno Dente and Francesco Kjellberg, eds. *The Dynamics of Institutional Change:Local Government Reorganization in Western Democracies* (London: SAGE, 1988)

SLACK, Enid and Richard BIRD, "Financing Urban Growth through Development Charges," *Canadian Tax Journal* Vol. 39, no. 5 (1991), pp. 1288-1304

SMALLWOOD, Frank, *Greater London: The Politics of Metropolitan Reform* (Indianapolis: Bobbs-Merrill, 1965)

STEPHENS, G. Ross and Nelson WIKSTROM, *Metropolitan Government and Governance: Theoretical Perspectives, Empirical Analysis, and the Future* (New York: Oxford University Press, 2000)

STEVENSON, Don, and Richard GILBERT, "Restructuring Municipal Government in Greater Toronto," prepared for the city of Montreal, 30 July 1999

STUDENSKI, Paul, *The Government of Metropolitan Areas in the United States* (New York: National Municipal League, 1930)

TEAFORD, Jon C., *City and Suburb: The Political Fragmentation of Metropolitan America, 1850-1970* (Baltimore: Johns Hopkins University Press, 1979)

THATCHER, Margaret, *The Downing Street Years* (New York: HarperCollins, 1993)

THOMAS, Hugh, letter to Tony Clement and attachment dated 25 November 1999 (the report of the special advisor for municipal restructuring in Sudbury)

TIERNEY, John, "Brooklyn Could Have Been a Contender," *The New York Times Magazine*, 28 December 1997

TORONTO, 1998 budget <http://www.city.toronto.on.ca/ourcity/budgets/operating99/bud_pres/sld008.htm>

TORONTO, Office of the Chief Administrative Officer, *Building the New City of Toronto: CAO's Mid-term Report to the Mayor and Members of Council*, July 1999

TORONTO, Office of the Chief Administrative Officer, Amalgamation Office, *Building the New City of Toronto: Status Report on Amalgamation*, July 1999

TORONTO STAR

TULLOCK, Gordon, *The New Federalist*, adapted for Canadian readers by Filip Palda (Vancouver: The Fraser Institute, 1994)

UMA GROUP IN ASSOCIATION WITH DOANE RAYMOND, *Analysis of Municipal Amalgamation*, prepared for The City of Halifax, The City of Dartmouth, The Town of Bedford and Halifax County Municipality, 12 April 12, 1995

UNITED KINGDOM, Royal Commission on Local Government in England, *Report*, Cmnd. 4040 (London: Her Majesty's Stationary Office, 1969)

UNITED KINGDOM, Royal Commission on Local Government in England, *Economies of Scale in Local Government Services*, Research Study 3, Cmnd. 4040-II (London: Her Majesty's Stationary Office, 1969)

UNITED STATES, Advisory Council on Intergovernmental Relations, *Metropolitan Organization: The St. Louis Case*, Report M-181(1988)

UNITED STATES, Advisory Council on Intergovernmental Relations, *Metropolitan Organization: The Allegheny County Case*, Report M-181 (1992), p.16

UNITED STATES, federal census: <http:www.census.gov/Press-Release/metro01.prn> and <http://www.gov/statab/ccdb301.txt>

UNITED STATES, Department of Commerce, U.S. Census Bureau, *1997 Census of Governments, vol. 1, Government Organization* (August 1999)

VINCE, Anne, "Amalgamations" in Brian Dollery and Neil Marshall, eds., *Australian Local Government: Reform and Renewal* (Melbourne: Macmillan Education Australia, 1997)

VOJNOVIC, Igor, *Municipal Consolidation in the 1990s: An Analysis of Five Canadian Municipalities* (Toronto: ICURR Press, 1997)

WALMSLEY, Ann, "City Lights," *The Globe and Mail Report on Business Magazine*, (August 1993)

WARNER, Sam Bass, Jr., *The Private City: Philadelphia in Three Periods of its Growth* (Philadelphia: University of Pennsylvania Press, 1968)

WEIGLEY, Russell F., "The Border City in Civil War, 1854-1865" in Russell. F. Weigley, ed., *Philadelphia: A 300-Year History* (New York: W.W. Norton, 1982)

WILLIAMS, Robert J. and Terrence J. DOWNEY, "Reforming Rural Ontario," *Canadian Public Administration* 42-2 (Summer 1999), 160-92

WINNIPEG, "Organizational Review and Performance Assessment Report," 29 October 1997 <http:www.mbnet.mb.ca/city/cuff.htm>